Three Prophets of Religious Liberalism:
CHANNING-EMERSON-PARKER

Three Prophets of Religious Liberalism:

CHANNING-EMERSON-PARKER

Second Edition

Introduced by Conrad Wright

Boston: Unitarian Universalist Association

First published by Beacon Press in 1961
Second Edition 1986

A Skinner House book published under the
auspices of the Unitarian Universalist Association
by arrangement with Beacon Press.

Printed in the United States of America

ISBN #0-933840-20-9

Note: The Unitarian Universalist Association is committed to using gender-inclusive language in all of its publications. In this edition the editor's introduction has been revised to conform to gender-inclusive usage. In the interest of historical authenticity quoted matter and the text of the Channing and Parker sermons and the Emerson address are printed, as in previous editions of this work, in their original form.

Contents

Three Prophets of Religious Liberalism:
CHANNING-EMERSON-PARKER

Introduction by Conrad Wright

I

Channing's Baltimore Sermon, Emerson's Divinity School Address, and Parker's South Boston Sermon have long been accepted as the three great classic utterances of American Unitarianism. Other comparable addresses have sometimes been nominated for inclusion in the canon of Unitarian scripture, but in the sifting and winnowing processes of time the acknowledged position of these three addresses has remained secure.

What do they have in common to account for their recognized standing? In the first place, they all occasioned widespread controversy. Channing's sermon of 1819 provided the liberal Christians of his day with a party platform, thereby sharpening the cleavage between them and their orthodox neighbors both theologically and ecclesiastically. The pamphlet warfare he initiated continued for half a decade, and the effects were lasting on Unitarians and Trinitarians alike. Emerson's address in 1838 similarly spoke for a new generation and stimulated reply and counterthrust by others, which continued long after Emerson himself had withdrawn from the debate. Parker's sermon in 1841 reinforced the reverberations of Emerson's address and was no less bitterly attacked and warmly defended. All three were significant for what they said but no less important for the response they elicited.

In the second place, all three of these addresses represent turning points in the history of American Unitarianism. Channing took the liberal wing of New England congregationalism, fastened a name to it, and forced it to overcome its reluctance to recognize that it had become, willy-nilly, a separate and distinct Christian body. Emerson cut deeply at the traditional philosophical presuppositions of the Unitarianism of his day, so that it was never thereafter possible for Unitarians to return

3

to the position that Christianity is based on the authority of Christ as the unique channel of God's revelation to humanity. Emerson and Parker alike insisted that the religious impulse is primary and universal and that Christianity is but one of many expressions of that primary impulse, deriving its authority from its congruity with universal truths. Since that time, there has always been a universalistic as well as a Christian component in American Unitarian thought; and much of the intellectual history of the denomination has involved the interplay between these two strands.

Finally, all three of these addresses were influential far beyond the confines of the religious body which produced them. This was especially true of the Divinity School Address. It is admittedly impossible to measure precisely the effect of this discourse in shaping the religious views of many who never became Unitarians and who may never have realized that Emerson's doctrine was rooted in Unitarianism. But this address is as much a classic of American as of Unitarian literature, and its influence has been correspondingly widespread and continuous. Parker's influence, also, was felt beyond the bounds of Unitarianism, reaching many for whom none of the traditional versions of Christianity, even liberal Christianity, had any attraction.

It may indeed be argued that the reputation of Channing, Emerson, and Parker beyond the confines of Unitarianism itself is the explanation for the special position of their three most influential addresses within the denomination. There were other sermons and pamphlets which also marked turning points in Unitarian history. Henry W. Bellows' *Suspense of Faith* (1859) was a call for self-appraisal, which led to a reinvigorated Unitarianism based on denominational organization after the Civil War. Jabez T. Sunderland's pamphlet, *The Issue in the West* (1886), which threatened to divide the denomination, led to a clearer understanding between conservative and radical Unitarians and ultimately to a reconciliation based on W. C. Gannett's "Things Commonly Believed Among Us." The "Humanist Manifesto" (1933) restated for its day the radical half of Unitarian doctrine. But while these publications attracted attention and aroused controversy, it was within the denomination itself that their influence was chiefly felt.

Hence the circumstances which made classics of the three earlier discourses may not soon recur. Channing's audience was concentrated and identifiable, so that its response might be calculated in advance; today it would be diffused and anonymous. Emerson's audience responded alertly to the doctrinal implications of his poetic utterance; today it would concern itself but casually with theological issues, no matter how basic, since we now use a secular rather than a theological vocabulary when issues really seem worth arguing about. Parker's sermon was addressed to Unitarians, but it created a sensation largely because the orthodox of that day were watching and listening and were insistent that the liberals either accept or disavow this strange new heresy; today a comparable sermon would pass unnoticed by other denominations, so pluralistic has our society become.

Until such time, therefore, as the denomination of Channing, Emerson, and Parker shall produce a prophet who can, like them, speak both to a parochial audience and to a universal one, the addresses here reprinted will stand alone, and their authors will remain the three stars of the first magnitude that American Unitarianism has produced.

II

Two kinds of epoch-making addresses may be distinguished. There is, on the one hand, the speech innocently delivered, with no thought that it will prove to be memorable. Thus the Gettysburg Address has lived while the major oration of that occasion has been forgotten. But there is also the address which is made memorable, at least in part, because those who planned the occasion were resolved that it should be made so. Channing's Baltimore Sermon falls into this latter category. "Attending circumstances," remarked one of the participants in the ceremonies of which Channing's sermon was the climax, give them "a vast solemnity and weight."[1] The address was memorable partly because the persons involved were determined, by a conscious, deliberate act, to make it a manifesto to which the religious community would have to give heed. It was not the isolated utterance of an individual but a party proclamation; and as such, it proved to be as brilliantly successful as its promoters could have hoped.

What was the party of which this sermon was the manifesto? Its members referred to themselves as "liberal Christians," and their territory of greatest influence was eastern Massachusetts. They were the heirs of two generations of theological liberals who had rejected New England Calvinism and rewritten Christian theology to conform to the rational doctrines and tolerant spirit of the Age of Reason. They were the intellectual successors of such men as Charles Chauncy, who was Jonathan Edwards' most persistent opponent at the time of the Great Awakening; Jonathan Mayhew, one of the first ministers in New England to reject the doctrine of the Trinity; John Tucker of Newbury, vigorous advocate of the free mind, unbound by creeds or confessions of faith; and Jeremy Belknap, whose historical researches declared his conviction that the clergy were as much responsible for the nourishment of humane letters as of theological speculation.

The liberal Christians included the ministers of the most influential churches of Boston and nearby towns: Channing himself, at the Federal Street Church, where his intense spirituality found expression in a pulpit manner and form of address that stirred his listeners almost to the point of idolatry; James Freeman of the Stone Chapel, who had led the oldest Episcopal church in Boston into anti-trinitarian congregationalism; Aaron Bancroft of Worcester, the father of an American diplomat and man of letters; and Charles Lowell, the father of another. In the congregations of such men were to be found the merchants, doctors, lawyers, and leaders of the commu-

---

[1] Nathaniel Thayer, "Address to the Society," in W. E. Channing, *A Sermon Delivered at the Ordination of the Rev. Jared Sparks* (Boston, 1819), p. 32.

nity, characterized by one of the orthodox ministers as "a formidable host . . . combining wealth, talents and influence."[2] Theirs was doubtless the confined stage of a provincial society; but within its limits, they were accustomed to exercise power and to make the decisions by which the communities of which they were the leading citizens were shaped.

It was something of an accident of history that these liberal Christians eventually came to be known as Unitarians. Anti-trinitarian they were, to be sure; but they long refused the Unitarian label, since at that time it connoted a variety of anti-trinitarianism which most of them rejected. Furthermore, their basic disagreement with orthodoxy was over human nature and the doctrines of grace, rather than over the doctrine of the Trinity. Calvinism asserted that the innate bent of all creatures is toward sin; that by an eternal decree God has predestined some to everlasting happiness and others to eternal torment; and that salvation comes to the elect as the unmerited gift of God's Holy Spirit. The liberals, on the other hand, believed that men and women are born with a capacity both for sin and for righteousness; that they can respond to the impulse toward holiness as well as to the temptation to do evil; and that life is a process of trial and discipline, by which, with the assistance God freely gives to all, the bondage to sin may gradually be overcome. This view of human nature and human destiny, referred to in those days as "Arminianism," was more optimistic than Calvinism, with its doctrines of original sin, election, and predestination. But it was a qualified and moderate optimism, as contrasted with later Unitarian assertions of the essential dignity of human nature, or Transcendentalist proclamations of the infinity of the soul.

Although a cleavage between the Calvinist and the Arminian wings of New England congregationalism may be traced back at least as far as the 1740's, an open breach did not appear until 1805. Down to that date, despite recurrent debate and disagreement, traditional acts of fellowship be-

[2] Jedidiah Morse, *An Appeal to the Public* (Charlestown, 1814), p. vi.

tween ministers of the two groups were not abandoned. Orthodox ministers still exchanged pulpits with their liberal colleagues and did not scruple to participate with them in ordinations and installations. Early in 1805, however, Henry Ware of Hingham, one of the liberals, was elected Hollis Professor of Divinity at Harvard, despite the strident protests of the orthodox. This election was the signal to the orthodox that control of the college had passed from their hands. The growing strength of the liberal Christians seemed all too freely exercised; and prominent orthodox ministers, like Jedidiah Morse of Charlestown, decided that the only way to defend orthodoxy was to isolate the liberal Christians and thereby restrict their influence.

Morse was by all odds the most energetic and effective leader of the orthodox. His situation was complicated, however, by the existence of divisions within the orthodox camp itself. Out of the theological speculations of Jonathan Edwards and Samuel Hopkins there had emerged certain doctrinal innovations within the framework of Calvinism, commonly referred to as the "New Divinity," or "Hopkinsianism." Many moderate Calvinists, at least in eastern Massachusetts, were as distrustful of the New Divinity as they were of Arminianism. Morse's grand strategy called for a reconciliation between moderate Calvinists and Hopkinsians, as well as a separation between them and the liberals. Although he failed in an attempt to organize a General Association of Ministers on orthodox principles, he was the key figure in drawing together the Hopkinsians and the moderate Calvinists in support of Andover Theological Seminary, founded in 1808. He also persuaded the two factions to merge their rival magazines. At the same time, the evangelical ministers began to limit their pulpit exchanges to members of their own group, even though this often meant the disruption of friendly relationships of long standing.

The years following the election of Henry Ware were punctuated by a series of dramatic conflicts. In 1808, John Codman's decision to restrict his exchanges resulted in a bitter struggle in the Second Church in Dorchester, which attracted widespread attention and intensified party alignments generally. In 1815, Jedidiah Morse discovered in the biography of an English Unitarian clergyman evidence sufficient to convince him not only that the New England liberals were more unorthodox than they were willing to acknowledge but that they were engaging in a dishonest conspiracy of silence. In order to smoke out the opposition, Morse reprinted the crucial chapter of the biography in pamphlet form, with introductory comments intended to prove that the liberal Christians were really Unitarians in the English sense of the term. This publication was promptly reviewed by one of Morse's parishioners, who called upon the orthodox to separate in worship and communion from the liberals.

Repeatedly the liberals protested against this "system of exclusion," as Channing termed it. The honor of religion, he declared, "can never suffer by admitting to Christian fellowship men of irreproachable lives, whilst it has suffered most severely from that narrow and uncharitable spirit which has excluded such men for imagined errors." The cause of truth, he continued, "can never suffer by admitting to Christian fellowship, men who honestly profess to make the Scriptures their rule of faith and practice, whilst it has suffered most severely by substituting for this standard, conformity to human creeds and formularies."[3] The consequence could only be the destruction of the traditional ecclesiastical institutions of New England, accompanied by bitterness and factional strife that would separate friends, divide churches, and even embitter family relationships.

By 1819, however, the liberals were forced to acknowledge that the situation would have to be accepted for what it was, and that, like it or not, they were becoming a distinct religious body. Channing's Baltimore Sermon contributed much to this process of self-discovery. Preached as it was by the most eloquent of the Boston ministers, who was known to deplore the sectarian spirit, its influence was incalculable.

[3] *The Works of William Ellery Channing, D.D.* (Boston, 1841), V, 376.

If Channing was ready to call himself a Unitarian, lesser ministers were emboldened to follow. The activities of Jedidiah Morse forced the liberals to become a separate denomination; but it was Channing who persuaded them to accept this unwelcome distinction and gave them a party platform on which to stand.

It is worthy of comment that this party proclamation of the New England liberals was delivered in Baltimore, rather than in Boston. For this occasion, which was regarded by the participants as having especial solemnity and weight, half a dozen of the most prominent Boston ministers had to travel four hundred miles from home. Some of them preached along the way—in New York, where a Unitarian church soon resulted, and in Philadelphia, where a struggling Unitarian church inspired by Joseph Priestley had been in existence for some years. The episode takes on the aspect of a foray of the leading Boston liberals into foreign territory. It has therefore a double significance: it signalized the acceptance by the liberals of their own distinctive theological and ecclesiastical position at home; it also declared their intention to carry the gospel of liberal Christianity to other parts of the land as well.

Although the ordination of Jared Sparks was the occasion for the first full-scale expedition of Boston Unitarianism beyond its original limits, preliminary scouting parties had already sent back intelligence reports as to the prospects in various cities along the eastern seaboard. In October, 1816, James Freeman conducted services in Baltimore in a hired hall. The response may be judged from a letter written by Edward Hinkley to his college chum, Jared Sparks, then engaged in theological studies. "For some time past," he wrote, "the theological doctors here have been making a great outcry against Unitarians and Unitarianism, that 'star in the North of ill omen,' as I heard Duncan call it. Dr. Freeman preached three Sundays in this city. Though he was obliged to preach in a ball-room, he had a large and respectable audience."[4]

[4] Herbert B. Adams, *The Life and Writings of Jared Sparks* (Boston and New York, 1893), I, 126.

Hinkley went on to say that one minister threatened to excommunicate any member of his church who went to hear Freeman but that plans were already being made for the construction of a Unitarian meetinghouse.

The years 1817 and 1818 saw Unitarianism in Baltimore in the process of organization. The First Independent Church of Baltimore was formed early in 1817; the cornerstone of its building was laid in June of that year, and the dedication exercises were held in October, 1818. Meanwhile, Hinkley had suggested to the promoters of the new enterprise that Sparks was "exactly the man" for them and had urged Sparks to come if called. "The parish will, I think, be large, and will, I know, be rich and respectable. . . . Mr. Williams tells me that as to the salary, $1,500 is the least sum that will be at first offered, that in case the minister should marry $2,000, with a dwelling, will be given." As for opposition, he reported, little need be feared. "At first a few of the ministers might preach a sermon or two to prove the trinity, &c., and some bigots might call a Unitarian an *infidel,* or *deist,* &c. But this sort of talk would be harmless to all but its authors, and would vanish 'like the morning cloud or the early dew.'"[5]

In the fall of 1818, Sparks was invited to Baltimore to preach as a candidate. In his letters home, he was frank enough to admit that his pulpit delivery had not met with entire approval: "My speaking has been severely criticised and found fault with, but my sermons, as my best friends tell me, have given universal satisfaction."[6] He received a unanimous call, in any event, and in February, 1819, set out for Boston to make arrangements for the ordination.

In a letter to Sparks, soon after his departure, one of the trustees of the church stressed the advantage in having the ordination "got up with some considerable shew of strength."[7] In Baltimore, the trustees went ahead with plans for newspaper publicity and worked on arrangements so that "such a

---

[5] *Ibid.,* I, 127, 128.
[6] *Ibid.,* I, 136–37.
[7] Charles H. Appleton to Sparks, February 23, 1819. MS., Harvard College Library.

force of talents" as was expected for the ordination might be
made available for other preaching engagements as well, and
thereby be put on display to the advantage of the cause. In
Boston, John Gorham Palfrey, a classmate of Sparks and the
minister of the Brattle Street Church, welcomed him with a
dinner party; and it is plausible to assume that the plans for
the ordination came under discussion. A closely knit group of
ministers, many of them intimate friends or sponsors of
Sparks, then dominated both the pulpits of Boston and the
government of Harvard College, so there was very much the
atmosphere of a caucus about the whole proceedings. Of those
invited to participate—one might almost say, designated to
participate—four were leading Boston ministers: Channing
and Palfrey, who made the trip, and Charles Lowell and Henry
Ware, Jr., who found it necessary to beg off. The Harvard
influence was especially marked: Channing and Eliphalet Por-
ter of Roxbury were both Fellows of the Corporation, while
Dr. Henry Ware was the Hollis Professor. President Kirkland
himself, although not to be present at the ordination in May,
was already helping by supplying the Baltimore pulpit for part
of the time during Sparks' absence.

  The ordination took place on May 5, 1819, and reports
quickly got back to Boston as to the events of the day. The
most detailed account, in a letter from Samuel A. Eliot to
Andrews Norton, conveys something of the sense of excite-
ment that prevailed among those present, confident as they
were that they were sharing in an historic occasion. "Wednesday at about ½ past 10," he wrote, "the services commenced,
& every body was very much interested & pleased. . . . The
sermon was an hour & a half long, & was an effort of uncom-
mon boldness & decision for Mr. Channing." The preacher's
manner was "more than usually animated." Mr. Palfrey's right
hand of fellowship and Dr. Ware's ordaining prayer were sin-
gled out for special praise. Eliot felt that he had never attended
a more interesting ordination service; it was "well worth coming 400 miles for, at least that & what was connected with it."
Certainly, he felt, the advance of truth in Baltimore was very

perceptible, "notwithstanding the violent efforts of the clergy to obstruct it."[8]

And so the group slowly dispersed homeward. On the way, Channing preached in New York, with the result that the First Congregational Society was organized there that very month. In Boston, the success of the expedition was the chief topic of conversation among the liberals. "The gentlemen who assisted at Mr. Sparks' ordination have returned," wrote Andrews Norton; "those whom I have seen, in fine spirits, and full of hope that correct opinions and feelings on the subject of religion will be more and more extended. Mr. Channing's sermon is said to have been a very eloquent and able exposition and defence of the principles of rational Christians."[9] Stephen Higginson, Jr., the steward of Harvard College, was even more exhilarated over the prospects. "Our success in New York," he wrote to Sparks, "proves the correctness of my view as it regards that city & we should now spare no pains to supply them with preaching. . . . Next comes Hartford, Washington & Richmond—& we must not sleep at our posts till the Truth is *openly* advocated in all our great cities."[10]

In Baltimore, Sparks promptly arranged for publication of Channing's sermon, and it was available in less than a month. A second Baltimore edition was required almost at once; and two editions, one of them unauthorized, were quickly issued in Boston. So great was the demand that it has been asserted that no pamphlet, save only Tom Paine's *Common Sense,* had ever before circulated so widely in this country.

The Baltimore Sermon has sometimes been interpreted as an appeal for the use of reason in religion and as a condemnation of the popular orthodoxy of the day on the grounds of

[8] Samuel A. Eliot to Andrews Norton, May 6, 1819. MS., Harvard College Library.

[9] Andrews Norton to George Bancroft, May 24, 1819. MS., Harvard College Library.

[10] Stephen Higginson, Jr., to Jared Sparks, May 19, 1819. MS., Harvard College Library.

promoted rationalism but ultim. Source = Scripture
some relig truths can be figured out, but some like
mediating role of JC, must learn f. Bible

14   Introduction

its irrationality. It is true that Channing believed that human
reason can and must be used to establish certain basic truths
of religion, such as the existence of God. But it is important
to note that the thrust of the Baltimore Sermon is in quite a
different direction. For Channing, as for the other liberals, the
unassisted reason can establish doctrines of natural religion.
But these doctrines must be supplemented by a special revelation, which is to be found in the Scriptures of the Old and
New Testaments: "Whatever doctrines seem to us to be clearly
taught in the Scriptures, we receive without reserve or exception." The distinctive doctrines of Christianity, such as the
mediatorial role of Jesus Christ, could never have been established by the unassisted reason. Channing was sensitive to the
charge that the liberals exalted reason above revelation, and
the Baltimore Sermon made a special point of refuting that
charge. Properly understood, it is a reminder that Unitarianism
began as a biblical faith.

To be sure, Channing declared that reason must be used
in the interpretation of Scripture; and he had a sublime confidence that no scriptural doctrine, rightly interpreted, will be
found to be irrational. But for him, as for earlier anti-trinitar-
ians, the conclusive argument for rejection of the doctrine of
the Trinity was that it is unscriptural. Accordingly, the theme
of the Baltimore Sermon is that the Scriptures, correctly interpreted, teach the doctrines of the liberal Christians, or Unitarians. Modern Unitarianism has moved so far from its
original biblical basis that we are likely to underestimate its
importance for Channing. He did not argue from Scripture, as
one might be tempted to suppose, simply for purposes of
strategy in opposing the orthodox of that day. He argued from
Scripture because, for him as for the other liberals, the Bible
was the sole source of Christian truth.

The main ideas of the Baltimore Sermon are arranged
under two headings. The first section outlines the principles
to be adopted in the interpretation of the Scriptures; the second part deals with certain doctrines which the Scriptures, so
interpreted, are found to contain. While the first section is the

shorter, it is perhaps the more significant of the two, for it is a brief statement of methods of biblical criticism then regarded as novel, if not revolutionary. Stimulated by a sudden awareness of the riches of German critical scholarship, the liberals were trying to master new principles of biblical study. Their intellectual horizons had suddenly widened, and they were confident that new ways were opening before them for the solution of perennially intractable theological problems. No small part of the enthusiasm with which they attacked orthodoxy stemmed from their confidence that the science of biblical criticism assured the ultimate triumph of liberal Christianity.

The new principles of biblical scholarship for which Channing was an advocate must be seen against the background of an earlier tradition of scriptural interpretation. In the eighteenth century, the liberals were wont to complain that the orthodox, and especially the evangelical revivalists, were constructing Christian doctrine on the basis of isolated verses of the Bible wrenched entirely out of context. Any kind of absurdity, they complained, can be demonstrated on the basis of isolated prooftexts. The only proper method of determining what the Bible teaches on a given point is to collect all the relevant passages and compare them one with another. This was the method used by the English philosopher Samuel Clarke in his *Scripture Doctrine of the Trinity* (1712) and by the dissenting minister John Taylor of Norwich in his *Scripture-Doctrine of Original Sin* (1740). Charles Chauncy in turn copied Taylor's methods and applied them to the doctrine of universal salvation in *The Salvation of All Men* (1784). The purpose in each case was to let obscure texts be clarified by clear and unambiguous ones; to allow the bold and unqualified language of one verse to be limited by the cautious phrasing of another; and to discover the inner logical consistency of the Scriptures which must pervade the whole, despite possible surface contradictions.

From the point of view of Channing's generation, the limitations of Clarke's method of scriptural interpretation were

obvious. It assumed that the Bible itself provides the key to
its own interpretation and, in theory at least, that every verse
of the Bible is of equal validity. It rejected the notion that
individual verses of the Bible can be understood in isolation
from the whole tenor of Scripture; but it assumed that the
Bible itself can be understood in isolation from the historical
circumstances that produced it. And so the Baltimore Sermon
emphasizes that "the Bible is a book written for men, in the
language of men," and—to use a modern expression—limited
by the culture that produced it. The Bible cannot be understood without a knowledge of the original tongues in which it
was composed, the culture of the Jewish people and the special
historical circumstances that occasioned particular books, and
even the quirks of personality of some of the authors. Isolated
passages of the Bible may be subject to a variety of alternative
interpretations; the only way to determine which one is correct
is to select "that which accords with the nature of the subject
and the state of the writer, with the connexion of the passage,
with the general strain of Scripture, with the known character
and will of God, and with the obvious and acknowledged laws
of nature." In short, in the Bible, the revelation of God is
refracted through human language and the circumstances of
human history. To understand God's will, we must make due
allowance for that refraction; and to that end, all the resources
of philology, of history, and of philosophy, both natural and
moral, must be brought to bear on the sacred texts.

Even among the liberals, Channing was neither the pioneer nor the foremost practitioner of these methods of biblical scholarship. The pioneer was perhaps Joseph Stevens
Buckminster, whose death in 1812 at the age of twenty-eight
cut short the career of a man regarded by his contemporaries
as the most brilliant and gifted of all the liberals of his generation. Buckminster's trip abroad in 1806 introduced him to a
new world of theological learning, and his library of more than
three thousand volumes, collected at that time, was one of the
vehicles by which the latest biblical scholarship was conveyed
to the New World. George Ticknor long afterwards declared

that it was Buckminster "who first took the critical study of
the Scriptures among us from the old basis . . . and placed it
on the solid foundations of the text of the New Testament as
settled by Wetstein and Griesbach, and elucidated by the la-
bors of Michaelis, Marsh, and Rosenmüller, and by the safe
and wise learning of Grotius, Le Clerc, and Simon." In brief,
Ticknor concluded, it has "hardly been permitted to any other
man to render so considerable a service as this to Christianity
in the Western World."[11]

If Buckminster was the pioneer, Andrews Norton was
without doubt the chief practitioner of the new scholarship.
His abilities were recognized as early as 1813, when he was
named Dexter Lecturer on Biblical Criticism at Harvard, an
appointment previously held by both Buckminster and Channing. In 1819, he became Dexter Professor of Sacred Literature, and his inaugural "Discourse on the Extent and Relations
of Theology" was in part a restatement of the principles of
criticism that bears comparison with Channing's sermon, delivered earlier the same year. As a teacher in the Divinity
School until 1830, he helped to shape a curriculum centered
in scriptural interpretation rather than dogmatic theology; and
as a leader of the Unitarian body until his death in 1853, he
stood for the most meticulous kind of scholarship and the
highest standard of professional integrity. In a sense, one
needs only to review the lifelong concerns and professional
achievement of Norton to understand what Channing was driv-
ing at in the first section of the Baltimore Sermon.

The second part of Channing's sermon, actually more
than twice the length of the first, is devoted to an exposition
of some of the doctrines to be derived from the Bible, "particularly those which distinguish us from other Christians."
The first of these is the Unity of God, as contrasted with the
doctrine of the Trinity. Next is the Unity of Christ, in place
of the doctrine of two natures in one person. The third point
is the moral perfection of God, whose infinite goodness, jus-

---

[11] George Ticknor, "Memoirs of the Buckminsters," *Christian
Examiner,* XLVII (1849), 186.

tice, and mercy manifest his concern for the virtue and happiness of human beings. The Calvinistic doctrines of depravity,
election, and eternal damnation are rejected as offering a false
and dishonorable view of God. The fourth doctrine is the
mediation of Christ: Channing acknowledges the existence of
some differences of opinion among Unitarians on this score;
but he insists that any doctrine of the atonement that implies
that the death of Jesus was necessary to placate an angry God
is absurd, unscriptural, and immoral. Finally, Channing ex-
plores the nature of true holiness, which he defines as love to
God, love to Christ, and benevolence toward one's fellow
human beings.

It is worth noting that while Channing's point with respect to these doctrines is that they are scriptural, he does not
actually attempt to prove that they are so. This part of the
sermon is not a demonstration of how the new principles of
interpretation should be applied; it is rather a statement, offered without proof, of the conclusions that result when those
principles are applied. Even the Note which Channing ap-
pended to the second edition of the sermon makes only a bare
beginning in the direction of proof. This was, after all, an
ordination sermon, not an introduction to the study of the
New Testament; and it was quite long enough as it stood, even
for a generation that did not boggle at lengthy discourses. For
the detailed analysis which Channing did not give, one has to
turn to certain of the controversial pamphlets published later
that year. Most notable of these was Andrews Norton's reply
to Moses Stuart's critique of Channing's sermon. Norton's
tract was entitled "Statement of Reasons for Not Believing
the Doctrines of Trinitarians" and was initially published in
the *Christian Disciple*; in this form, it was sixty-four pages
long. A decade later, it was rewritten and enlarged to book
length. It was reprinted as late as 1859 and served as the
standard Unitarian treatment of the topic until a later generation of liberals lost interest in the original biblical basis for
anti-trinitarian theology

If Channing omitted exegesis and criticism from his sermon as ill suited to the occasion, he omitted other themes

because they were not matters of disagreement between the liberals and the orthodox. In particular, he passed over all discussion of natural religion, its relationship to revealed religion, and the problem of Christian evidences. These themes, which he handled elsewhere, notably in his Dudleian Lecture two years later, were as characteristic of the thought of the early Unitarians as the doctrines actually discussed in the Baltimore Sermon. They were not, however, the distinguishing doctrines of the liberals.

Furthermore, the emphasis which Channing placed on the doctrines of the Trinity and the dual nature of Christ may be somewhat misleading. As we have already seen, the most persistent and irreconcilable disagreement between the liberals and the orthodox was over the nature and destiny of humanity. Channing touched on these issues in dealing with the moral perfection of God; but his attack on Calvinism was much more oblique than it was in other writings of his, such as "The Moral Argument against Calvinism" (1820) and "Unitarian Christianity Most Favorable to Piety" (1826). In the pamphlet warfare in 1819 and 1820, for every interchange between Moses Stuart and Andrews Norton on the doctrine of the Trinity, there were three between Leonard Woods and Henry Ware on the doctrine of human nature. The imbalance in Channing's sermon was, in a sense, rectified in the pamphlets that followed.

The Baltimore Sermon must be read, therefore, as a typical, though incomplete, expression of the mind of the early Unitarians. But it is hardly fair to complain that Channing did not produce a *Summa Theologica* in twenty-five pages octavo. He set for himself a specific objective, and there was no doubt in the minds of most of his congregation on that Wednesday morning in May, 1819, that he had succeeded in doing precisely what he had set out to do.

III

In May, 1819, Ralph Waldo Emerson was still a student at Harvard College. His own minister was Channing, since his mother had taken up going to the Federal Street Church after the death of Emerson's father in 1811. Presumably he read Channing's sermon when it was fresh from the press; but we do not know what his reaction was, or the extent to which he shared in the excited discussions of the Baltimore expedition.

There was another occasion, however, when an address by Channing made a very deep impression on him. In March, 1821, Channing was the Dudleian Lecturer at Harvard, taking as his assigned topic "The Evidences of Revealed Religion." Emerson recalled the address vividly two years afterwards, when Channing dealt with the same subject in a Sunday sermon. "I heard Dr. Channing deliver a discourse upon Revelation as standing in comparison with Nature," he wrote. "I have heard no sermon approaching in excellence to this, since the Dudleian Lecture. . . . He considered God's word to be the only expounder of his works, and that Nature had always been found insufficient to teach men the great doctrines which Revelation inculcated." In April, 1824, when Emerson took account of himself, his talents and his failings, preparatory to beginning the professional study of theology, Channing's lecture came back to his mind as an example of the sort of reasoning he hoped to pursue. "Dr. Channing's Dudleian Lecture is the model of what I mean, and the faculty which produced this is akin to the higher flights of the fancy."[12]

Emerson's praise of this lecture serves as a reminder that at the beginning of his career he accepted without reservation the system of rational theology that prevailed among the Unitarians of that day. The Divinity School Address, in 1838, revealed the extent to which he had departed from that system; and the vigor of the response on the part of men like Andrews Norton indicated how much seemed to be at stake. Channing's Dudleian Lecture helps us to measure the distance Emerson moved in a decade and a half, as well as to appreciate the growing divergence between the generations for which the two men spoke.

[12] *The Journals of Ralph Waldo Emerson* (Boston, 1909–14), I, 290, 361.

Channing's concern in the Dudleian Lecture was to vindicate the miracles of Christ as confirmation of the supernatural basis of Christianity. "Christianity is not only confirmed by miracles," he declared, "but is in itself, in its very essence, a miraculous religion." He recognized a prevailing tendency, fostered by the discoveries of science, to deny that the uniform order of nature will ever be interrupted by supernatural agency, and he acknowledged that all claims for miracles must be more carefully sifted than would be necessary for reports of common facts. But one who believes in God, the author of the uniformity of nature, must admit that he has the power to suspend the laws he has himself ordained, if the great purposes of the universe are thereby promoted. The great end of God in establishing the order of nature is "to form and advance the mind"; and if that purpose can best be achieved by departing from this order, "then the great purpose of the creation, the great end of its laws and regularity, would demand such departure; and miracles, instead of warring against, would concur with nature."[13]

Admittedly, God will not suspend the order of nature for trivial ends. But in extraordinary circumstances, for extraordinary purposes, miracles may reasonably be expected. Such was the situation when Jesus Christ came into the world. Pagan superstition had so obscured the doctrine of one God, which is the basis for all piety, and pagan philosophy had so shaken the doctrine of immortality, which is the foundation of morality, that a miraculous manifestation of God's power was required. Jesus Christ was therefore divinely commissioned to recover humanity from darkness and folly, and to disclose the way to eternal life. The miracles were vivid confirmation of his unique authority.

Channing did not rest the argument for Christianity solely on the historical miracles of Christ. He was familiar with the other evidences commonly adduced by Christian apologists: the fulfillment of prophecy; the fitness of Christian truths to

[13] Channing, *Works*, III, 106, 112–13.

meet the needs of sinful creatures; the marvelous spread of Christianity, despite its appearance among obscure and humble people; the confirmation of the gospel history to be found in pagan writers; and so on. But in his Dudleian Lecture, he devoted more attention to the argument for miracles than to any of the other internal or external evidences; for there was a tendency among the liberal Christians to insist on the historicity of the miracles as the cornerstone of the whole structure of Christian apologetics.

The temper of Emerson's mind, as he himself realized, was more poetic or imaginative than strictly rational; and so Channing's lecture appealed to him because he detected in it a certain quality of "moral imagination" which set it apart from routine treatments of the same theme. Locke and Samuel Clarke, by comparison, he regarded as "reasoning machines." Yet in his early preaching, as minister of the Second Church in Boston, Emerson remained within the rationalistic tradition for which Locke and Clarke spoke. In a sermon preached in 1831, he declared that "a miracle is the only means by which God can make a communication to men, that shall be known to be from God," and that the New Testament miracles have a "peculiar credibility." To be sure, he was more inclined to prove the credibility of the miracles from the truth of the doctrines of the gospels than the other way around; and to this extent he was moving in the direction of the Divinity School Address. But in 1831, he believed that "the truth and the miracles mutually confirm each other," and he had as yet no other basis for religious truth than rational argument founded on the experience of the senses, together with special revelation attested by miracles.[14]

By 1834, Emerson had broken away from the old patterns of thought and had moved into a new intellectual climate in which the familiar arguments for miracles could be casually dismissed as irrelevant. In May of that year, in a letter to his brother, he used Coleridge's distinction between the "Reason"

[14] A. C. McGiffert, Jr. (ed.), *Young Emerson Speaks* (Boston, 1938), pp. 120, 123.

and the "Understanding," which seemed to him to be "a philosophy itself." Reason, he said—using the word in a way
peculiar to the Transcendentalists—is "the highest faculty of
the soul"; it is the power by which we apprehend truth immediately, without calculation or proof. The Understanding,
on the other hand, "toils all the time, compares, contrives,
adds, argues, near sighted but strong-sighted, dwelling in the
present the expedient the customary." On the level of the
Understanding, we have varying degrees of intellectual capacity; but "Reason is potentially perfect in every man." Our
everyday life may be lived on the level of the Understanding;
but our deepest insights into timeless truths are intuitions of
the Reason, and religion and poetry belong in its domain.[15]

The emergence of this intuitional philosophy led inevitably to conflict and crisis within the Unitarian community.
For more than a century, the accepted philosophy in New
England had been based either on the sensational psychology
of John Locke or on the modified Lockeanism of the Scotch
Realists. True ideas, said Locke, are based on the evidence
of the senses, as ordered and organized by the ability of the
mind to reflect on the ideas derived from sensations. But now
Emerson's generation was beginning to assert that the truths
of religion and morality are not founded on the experience of
the senses but are immediate intuitions of the divine. What
this meant to Unitarianism was sensed with especial clarity
by Convers Francis, minister of the church in Watertown. "I
have long seen," he wrote in 1836, "that the Unitarians must
break into two schools,—the Old one, or English school, belonging to the sensual and empiric philosophy,—and the New
one, or the German school (perhaps it may be called), belonging to the spiritual philosophy."[16] But if the spiritual or "transcendentalist" school should prevail and the truths of
Christianity be regarded as valid only so far as they correspond

[15] Ralph L. Rusk (ed.), *The Letters of Ralph Waldo Emerson*
(New York, 1939), I, 412–13.
[16] John Weiss, *Discourse Occasioned by the Death of Convers
Francis, D.D.* (Cambridge, 1863), pp. 28–29.

to direct intuitions of absolute truth, Jesus would lose his function as the unique channel of divine revelation, and the miracles wrought in confirmation of his authority would shrink into triviality.

Despite Channing's impatience with the tendency of Unitarianism to settle down into a new orthodoxy, and his generous tolerance of the views of the younger generation, his theological allegiance remained with the old school. Emerson's altered attitude toward him is a measure of the growing gulf between the generations. "Once Dr. Channing filled our sky," he wrote in 1837. "Now we become so conscious of his limits and of the difficulty attending any effort to show him our point of view that we doubt if it be worth while. Best amputate."[17]

If the Divinity School address was an event in the intellectual life of New England, it was also an event in the spiritual biography of its author. In his discussion of the role of the minister, addressed to young men about to enter the ministry, Emerson was struggling with his own vocational conflicts and doubts; and it may even be argued that he was indirectly justifying his own withdrawal from the calling to which he had been solemnly consecrated.

Emerson had once sought the "prized gown and band" because of his "passionate love for the strains of eloquence." Public preaching, he had decided, would give him an opportunity for the inspired utterance of which he felt himself capable. But he found much of drudgery in the minister's tasks, and the routine of parish calling in particular was uncongenial. Even before he resigned as minister of the Second Church, he had become restive, and critical of his own profession: "It is the best part of a man, I sometimes think, that revolts most against his being a minister." The difficulty was that ministers must accommodate themselves to institutions already formed, and each such accommodation is "a loss of so much integrity and, of course, of so much power."[18]

[17] Emerson, *Journals*, IV, 239.
[18] *Ibid.*, I, 363; II, 448–49.

Emerson's resignation was directly occasioned by a disagreement over the administration of the Lord's Supper; but his growing dissatisfaction with the ministry would doubtless have led to his withdrawal sooner or later. Yet he did not break completely with that profession. Following his return from Europe in 1833, he continued to do occasional preaching, and for about three years he served as "stated supply" at the church in East Lexington. He was gradually finding his way into a new career as lecturer, and it was only when he achieved some degree of public acceptance that he finally gave up the East Lexington pulpit. "But henceforth perhaps I shall live by lecturing which promises to be good bread," he wrote to his mother in March, 1838. "I have relinquished my ecclesiastical charge at E Lexington & shall not preach more except from the Lyceum."[19]

This decision was not an easy one for him to make. It involved the abandonment of the clerical tradition he had inherited; more painful, it amounted to an admission that the profession of the ministry made demands on him that he was unwilling or unable to meet. But he could not handle the situation in such a frank and undisguised form. Instead, he sought to justify himself by arguing that the church was tottering to its fall, almost all life extinct. In short, the blame for his failure as a minister lay not with himself but the institutions of organized religion, which he declared could no longer command respect.

On the Sundays when Emerson was not preaching at East Lexington, or elsewhere on exchange, he ordinarily attended church in Concord. There, in the preaching of the Rev. Barzillai Frost, Emerson found ample confirmation of what, for his own peace of mind, he had to believe. Frost was a graduate of the Divinity School in Cambridge and a firm believer in the historical argument for Christianity, based on the miracles. He was also a faithful parish minister, regularly discharging his pastoral duties and making the rounds of his three hundred families. But he was a mediocre preacher, as even

---

[19] *Letters* II, 120.

his best friend had to acknowledge. "Doubtless you all early felt," declared Henry A. Miles in a eulogy following Frost's death, "that there was neither flexibility of voice, nor play of imagination, nor gush of emotion to give him, as a preacher, that power to which other endowments fairly entitled him."[20] He wholly lacked the gift of eloquence, the power to change people's lives in an instant by the spoken word, that Emerson looked for in the true preacher. In short, he was a living example of all that Emerson thought was wrong with the clergy of his day.

Emerson's reaction to Frost's preaching, as the *Journals* reveal, was almost uniformly unfavorable. Time and again, he returned from church on Sunday morning to record his dissatisfaction. It is significant that the intensity of his criticism of Frost seems to have been greatest in March, 1838, just at the time that he was finally arranging to relinquish the East Lexington pulpit. After the decision had been made, and Emerson had solved the problem of his relationship to the profession for which Frost served as the symbol, the intensity of his condemnation perceptibly diminished.

The clustering of events is significant. It was on March 14 that Emerson wrote to his mother of his decision to quit his ecclesiastical charge. Sunday, the eighteenth, in a lengthy entry in the *Journal,* he condemned Frost as a sincere person based on sham; and he declared: "I ought to sit and think, and then write a discourse to the American Clergy, showing them the ugliness and unprofitableness of theology and churches at this day. . . ."[21] That same week, by a strange coincidence, he received a letter from a committee of the senior class of the Harvard Divinity School. Dated March 21, it invited him "to deliver before them, in the Divinity Chapel, on Sunday evening the 15th of July next, the customary discourse, on occasion of their entering upon the active Christian ministry."[22] The last Sunday at East Lexington was March 25. The

[20] Henry A. Miles, *A Sermon Preached . . . at the Burial of Rev. Barzillai Frost* (Cambridge, 1859), p. 9.
[21] *Journals,* IV, 413.
[22] *Letters,* II, 147 n.

following Tuesday, Emerson wrote to the committee to accept their invitation.

The address he carried with him to Cambridge, four months later, seemed to be an objective and impersonal report of the universal decay of faith, and a protest against the triumph of formalism in the pulpit. The text gave no hint of the fact that crucial passages condemning the clergy of the day had been drawn from Emerson's *Journals,* where in their original context they were references to the minister in Concord. Indeed, as the day for the delivery of the address drew near, Emerson was able to persuade himself that he was speaking "simple truth without any bias, any foreign interest in the matter."[23] But we are now able to discern what the audience of that day could not know, and Emerson himself could not admit: that there is a hidden meaning in the Divinity School Address, the clue to which lies in Emerson's relationship to his own minister and in the vocational crisis with which he was struggling.

The little chapel in Divinity Hall seats less than one hundred; and on the evening of July 15, all the places were taken. Edward Everett Hale, who arrived late, had to be content with a chair in the entry. We can list the names of perhaps a score of those present. Presumably six of the seven members of the graduating class were there; one of them, we know, was preaching in East Bridgewater. The members of the faculty were on hand, as well as a number of recent graduates of the School, such as Convers Francis, Caleb Stetson, Cyrus Bartol, William Henry Channing, John Sullivan Dwight, and Theodore Parker. Finally, there were young men, like Joseph Henry Allen, Rufus Ellis, and James H. Perkins, who were to enter the ministry in due course; and young women, like Elizabeth Peabody and Sarah Hale.

No detailed description of the order of exercises has come down to us. We do know that Emerson prefaced his remarks with a brief invocation, which Cyrus Bartol long after-

[23] *Journals,* V, 7.

wards recalled as follows: "We desire of the Infinite Wisdom and Goodness to be led into the Truth. So may it be by our lowliness and seeking! This we ask of the Infinite Wisdom and Goodness."[24] The burden of the address that followed was simple. It was a reminder that the life of religion must be re-created anew in the souls of each successive generation, and a declaration that it is the responsibility of the minister to "acquaint men at first hand with Deity." But Emerson was not content to state his position positively and let the matter rest. The corollary was explicitly stated, that the "great and perpetual office of the preacher" was not being discharged, and that there prevailed generally "a decaying church and a wasting unbelief."

The young transcendentalists in the audience were delighted by the performance. It is reported that Elizabeth Peabody was "enraptured." But many of those present were sharply critical, partly because of the ideas expressed, but also because they felt that Emerson had shown exceedingly poor taste in criticizing the clergy on such an occasion. They could hardly have been aware of the inner compulsion that had made him speak as he did. "I did not like it at all," wrote Edward Everett Hale. "Mr. E. held that the Christianity of the present day is little better than none; . . . that churchgoing was less popular than formerly, owing to the bad preaching of the ministers of the day, whom he rated severely as not putting enough of self into their sermons."[25] Hale's complaint that Emerson's strictures on the clergy were an insult to the Divinity School teachers who had trained them was echoed by his brother Nathan. "I didn't hear Emerson's lecture," he wrote, "& was very glad that I didn't, when I was told what it was. . . . It seems there were two divisions; the first asserting that *no* ministers of the present day (he made *no exceptions*) did their duty or did anything; doing away all the good the

---

[24] Cyrus A. Bartol, *Ralph Waldo Emerson* (Boston, 1882), p. 9.
[25] Jean Holloway, *Edward Everett Hale* (Austin, Texas, 1956), p. 40.

poor Divinity teachers hoped they had been doing for three years—the second was an express denial of *all* the divine claims of our Savior. . . ."[26]

After the exercises were over, the congregation broke up into small groups. Some of them walked over to Dr. Palfrey's house, where they lingered to talk. Henry Ware, Jr., invited Mr. and Mrs. Emerson to spend the night; but they preferred to drive back to Concord through the soft summer night, illuminated by a brilliant aurora. Before they left, however, Ware expressed to Emerson some of his uneasiness about the doctrines preached that evening; and Emerson seems to have reassured him by qualifying in conversation some of his bolder statements. The next day, however, Ware sought to make his position clear in a friendly letter. "It has occurred to me," he wrote, "that, since I said to you last night, I should probably assent to your unqualified statements, if I could take your qualifications with them, I am bound in fairness to add, that this applies only to a portion, and not to all. With regard to some, I must confess, that they appear to me more than doubtful, and that their prevalence would tend to overthrow the authority and influence of Christianity. On this account, I look with anxiety and no little sorrow to the course which your mind has been taking."[27]

The storm that blew up over the address seems to have come as a surprise to Emerson. This was no Baltimore Sermon, carefully calculated in advance to arouse controversy and to advance the principles of a party. And so, for a time, Emerson wondered whether the text should be revised before publication—or, indeed, whether it should be made available for general circulation at all. He finally concluded that he would have to stand or fall by what he had actually said, and so the Address appeared without significant revision late in August.

[26] Nathan Hale, Jr., to James Russell Lowell, July 24, 1838. MS., Harvard College Library.
[27] John Ware, *Memoir of the Life of Henry Ware, Jr.* (Boston, 1846), p. 395.

Inevitably it became a subject for public controversy as well as private conversation. From the point of view of the Divinity School authorities, the immediate problem was to make it plain that Emerson's views were his own and were not in any sense sanctioned by the School. The faculty felt that Emerson had placed them in a false light in the eyes of the public by choosing that particular platform and occasion for his remarks; and some of them wondered whether, in future years, the students should have complete freedom when it came to extending invitations to speak under the auspices of the School. Andrews Norton could not contain himself; he wrote an intemperate letter to a Boston newspaper to emphasize "the disgust and strong disapprobation" felt by the authorities. The members of the graduating class, he declared, "have become accessories, perhaps innocent accessories, to the commission of a great offence"; and he called upon them for whatever exculpation or excuse they could give.[28]

The more persistent issues, however, were doctrinal. One of them was posed by Henry Ware, Jr., in a sermon entitled "The Personality of the Deity," preached at the Divinity School on September 23, 1838. Although not a direct attack on Emerson, it was prepared with the Divinity School Address in mind. Ware was troubled by a prevailing tendency, of which Emerson's Address was but one instance, to think of God in terms of "divine laws" instead of as a Being who is at once Creator, Governor, and sustaining Parent. Emerson's assertion that "the soul knows no persons" seemed to him to be both theologically unsound and psychologically untrue. It is our concern for human personality that is the mainspring of progress in human affairs; and it is our response to a divine personality that is at the heart of worship. Ware was at least as much concerned as Emerson about the prevalence of moral and religious deadness; but, for him, the surest way to lose the sense of the presence of the Living God is to define religion as "a reverence and delight in the presence of certain divine

[28] Perry Miller, *The Transcendentalists* (Cambridge, 1950), p. 195.

laws." A relationship to an inanimate abstraction is not enough to satisfy the religious sentiments. Only as we "come more to realize the presence and the authority of the living Father" is there any grounds to hope for a "wider prevalence of elevated piety or of happy devotion to duty."[29]

The other doctrinal issue was the familiar one of the miracles. Emerson had long since made up his mind that converts to genuine Christianity are made by "the reception of beautiful sentiments, never by miracle."[30] And so he casually dismissed a doctrine that was regarded, by both Unitarians and orthodox, as essential to the acceptance of Christianity as a revealed religion. Jesus spoke of miracles, Emerson declared—playing on the word—"for he felt that man's life was a miracle, and all that man doth. . . . But the word Miracle, as pronounced by Christian churches, gives a false impression; it is Monster. It is not one with the blowing clover and the falling rain." Or, more pointedly: "To aim to convert a man by miracles is a profanation of the soul."

This heresy was not peculiar to Emerson. In 1836, George Ripley had bluntly declared in the *Christian Examiner* that "the design of the miracles, in the Old and New Testament, was not to confirm a revelation of spiritual truth, but to accomplish quite a different purpose."[31] Andrews Norton had reacted promptly by withdrawing as a sponsor of the magazine. That same year, William Henry Furness had argued that the so-called miracles of Jesus "were not departures from the laws of nature, but new facts in nature"; they were not performed "merely for the sake of the influence they might have on the understandings of others," but were "the simple, natural, irrepressible manifestations of that mighty spiritual force which was the inmost God-inspired life of Jesus."[32]

[29] *The Works of Henry Ware, Jr.* (Boston, 1847), III, 39.
[30] Emerson, *Journals,* IV, 429.
[31] George Ripley, "Martineau's *Rationale of Religious Enquiry,*" *Christian Examiner,* XXI (1836), 251.
[32] William Henry Furness, *Remarks on the Four Gospels* (Philadelphia, 1836), pp. 187, 199.

But Emerson's fault was that he had spoken on a public occasion under the auspices of the Divinity School. To Norton it seemed that a correspondingly important occasion was required for reply. The opportunity came a year later, at a meeting of the alumni of the School. Norton made no mention of Emerson in his "Discourse on the Latest Form of Infidelity" but attacked rather the tendency of certain German theologians to discount the evidential value of miracles. "The latest form of infidelity," he declared, "strikes directly at the root of faith in Christianity, and indirectly of all religion, by denying the miracles attesting the divine mission of Christ." No one had any doubt that Norton regarded Emerson as the leading local exponent of this position, or that he was addressing himself to Emerson when he insisted that "for any one to pretend to be a Christian teacher, who disbelieves the divine origin and authority of Christianity, and would undermine the belief of others, is treachery towards God and man."[33]

Emerson made public reply neither to Henry Ware, Jr., whom he held in the most affectionate regard, nor to Andrews Norton, whose dogmatic pronouncements he found thoroughly distasteful. The defense of the transcendentalist point of view was left to others, George Ripley and Theodore Parker in particular. But despite his aloofness from the controversy, Emerson was emotionally much more deeply involved in the whole episode than he was perhaps willing to admit. The Address, according to a recent scholar, "came as close to the irresistible truth he felt called upon to announce to his generation as any of his utterances. . . . He was correspondingly affected by its hostile reception." He was reminded that eloquence and poetic insight do not necessarily carry all before them. It was "an angular intrusion of fact into the smooth world of his thoughts" which permanently affected his philosophical outlook, at least to the extent that it forced him

---

[33] Andrews Norton, *A Discourse on the Latest Form of Infidelity* (Cambridge, 1839), pp. 11, 37.

thereafter to be more cautious in his proclamation of the identity of the ideal and the real.[34]

In time, the Unitarians abandoned the traditional theory
of miracles, as well as much of the theological structure built
upon it. Emerson and Ripley doubtless contributed to this
outcome. But even more important was the spread of a sci-
entific and critical attitude which was, in a somewhat different
way, as destructive of the older theology as was Transcendentalism. The Divinity School Address remains, therefore, a
perennially fresh solvent of dogmatic orthodoxies, especially
Unitarian orthodoxies, rather than an indication of the permanent philosophic bent of Unitarianism in this country.

IV

"The brilliant genius of Emerson rose in the winter
nights," Theodore Parker recalled, "and hung over Boston,
drawing the eyes of ingenuous young people to look up to that
great, new star, a beauty and a mystery. . . ."[35] In 1838, Parker
was himself just enough younger than Emerson to share something of this sense of wonder and delight in the appearance of
a nova in the sky. A recent graduate of the Divinity School,
Parker had been installed only a year earlier as minister of the
little church in West Roxbury. On July 15, after the usual
routine of preaching, Sunday school, and teachers' meeting,
Mrs. Parker and he proceeded by way of Brookline to Cambridge to hear Emerson. "I shall give no abstract," he wrote
in his *Journal,* "so beautiful, so just, so true, and terribly
sublime, was his picture of the faults of the Church in its
present position." To his classmate George Ellis he wrote: "It
was the noblest of all his performances: a little exaggerated,
with some philosophical untruths, it seemed to me; but the

[34] Stephen E. Whicher, *Freedom and Fate* (Philadelphia, 1953),
p. 73.
[35] *Theodore Parker's Experience as a Minister* (Boston, 1859),
p. 51.

noblest, the most inspiring strain I ever listened to." He returned to West Roxbury with his soul deeply stirred, and with
the resolution fixed afresh to prepare some long-meditated
sermons "on the state of the Church and the duties of these
times."[36] .

Parker followed with interest the ensuing controversy
between Norton and Ripley. Although he had the greatest
respect for the accuracy and depth of Norton's biblical scholarship, his sympathies were entirely with the Transcendentalists. He felt, however, that there was "a higher word to be
said on this subject" than Ripley was disposed to say; and so
he, too, entered the discussion with a pamphlet, published
under the pseudonym of "Levi Blodgett." Norton and Ripley
were debating the question "Do men believe in Christianity
solely on the ground of miracles?" But there is a previous
question, Parker urged, that must first be settled: "How do
men come to have any religion, or, in other words, *on what
evidence do they receive the plainest religious truths?*"[37]

For his part, Parker insisted that human beings are by
nature religious, that they are "made to be religious, as much
as an ox was made to eat grass." Hence the existence of God
is not something that we must discover, as the more conservative Unitarians supposed, by a process of reasoning, or by
a long series of deductions from facts experienced by the
senses. It is "a truth fundamental in our nature; given outright
by God; a truth which comes to light as soon as self-con-
sciousness begins." Our concept of the nature of God and the
divine attributes is developed by the Understanding; but prior
to the shaping of that concept, and of a higher order of awareness, is the "instinctive intuition of the divine." Parker acknowledged that there is more than one way of communicating
with God, and he did not fail to mention the indirect ways by

---

[36] Octavius Brooks Frothingham, *Theodore Parker* (Boston,
1874), p. 106.

[37] Theodore Parker, "The Previous Question Between Mr. Andrews Norton and His Alumni Moved and Handled." Appendix to John
Edward Dirks, *The Critical Theology of Theodore Parker* (New York,
1948), pp. 138, 140.

which our sense impressions of the material universe may lead us there. But our highest and most permanent faculties, conscience, and the "religious sentiment," are channels of direct communication with God: "I can find nothing interposed between Conscience and God, or between Him and the religious Sentiment; we border closely upon God everywhere; here we touch and he interpenetrates us, if I may so speak." No external authority, no authentication by miracles, is required to convince us of the essential truth of religion: the existence of God, on whom we are dependent.[38]

But what of Christianity and the truths peculiar to it? These were the doctrines, after all, for which confirmation by miracles was demanded. Parker replied that if no miracle is needed to establish the primary and essential truths of religion, "no man can consistently demand a miracle as a proof that Christ spoke the truth when he taught doctrines of infinitely less importance, which were themselves unavoidable conclusions from these two admitted truths." Parker was willing to acknowledge that Jesus, "like other religious teachers," wrought miracles. Yet Christianity does not rest on miracles, but "on the truth of its doctrines, and its sufficiency to satisfy all the moral and religious wants of man."[39]

For Parker, the beauty and greatness of the religion of Jesus lay in its reaffirmation of the primary and essential truths of all religion. This does not mean, however, that he would have been content with an absolute religion from which all the historical particularity of Jesus had been purged. Great religious teachers are always needed to give us a renewed awareness of truths for which the ultimate sanction is, admittedly, our own religious sentiment. And so Parker gratefully acknowledged that he could conceive of "no more perfect moral and religious incarnation of God, than Jesus of Nazareth," and declared that "the Christianity of Christ is the purest, the most intense, and perfect religion ever realized on earth." Not the Christianity, he hastened to add, "of Calvin or Luther; of the

[38] *Ibid.*, pp. 140, 141, 145.
[39] *Ibid.*, pp. 151, 157.

Unitarians or the Quakers; of Paul, James or Peter or John,
all of which are obviously one-sided and in part false," but
the Christianity of Jesus.[40]

Parker's "Levi Blodgett Letter" seems to have attracted
little attention. It reveals, however, that, even before the
South Boston Sermon, Parker had worked his way into a new
world of theological discourse. The contrast between the transcendentalist Unitarianism of the "Levi Blodgett Letter" and
the rationalistic Unitarianism of a man like Andrews Norton
is obvious. For Norton, the focus of concern was the rational
appraisal of Christian evidences. For Parker, it was the instinctive intuition of the divine, which he identified with the religion
of Jesus.

Seen in the context of the broad philosophical alignments
of that day, Parker clearly belongs with Emerson and the
Transcendentalists. But Transcendentalism was a stream of
tendency, rather than a standardized body of thought; and
Parker's religious ideas were far from being a carbon copy of
Emerson's. For one thing, the tone of his religious emotions
was much more specifically Christian than Emerson's, and the
Christian Church had much more meaning for him. Emerson
could drift almost casually out of the ministry; Parker would
not let criticism, even ostracism, drive him from his post as
the minister of a Christian church. His impact on the Unitarian
community was correspondingly direct and specific. After
Emerson's withdrawal from the ministry, conservative Unitarians could assume that he spoke for himself alone, and
could dismiss his transcendental vagaries as of no immediate
concern. But Parker, who was in attitude and temperament
much closer to conservative Unitarianism than Emerson,
could not be so easily set aside. He remained a persistent
irritant within the Unitarian community; and he suffered the
customary fate of nonconformists who decline to withdraw
politely, despite pointed suggestions that they are not entirely
welcome.

[40] *Ibid.*, pp. 149, 150.

On May 19, 1841, a damp, raw Wednesday, Parker delivered the sermon at the ordination of Charles C. Shackford, at the Hawes Place Church in South Boston. The council for the ordination was by no means transcendentalist in complexion; it included such conspicuous leaders of old-school Unitarianism as Dr. John Pierce of Brookline, who gave the ordaining prayer, and Samuel K. Lothrop of the Brattle Street Church, who delivered the charge to the minister.

It is not wholly clear why Parker was invited to preach on this occasion. Shackford was a graduate of Harvard College, class of 1835; but his theological inclinations at first were orthodox, rather than Unitarian, and he studied at Union and Andover seminaries, instead of the Harvard Divinity School. If he had any great sympathy for transcendentalist theology, he gave no public indication of it, then or later. Nor does there seem to be any reason to place him among Parker's close friends. It was asserted at the time that the selection had been made by a committee of the church rather than by Shackford, though of course the choice would necessarily have had Shackford's assent.

Whatever may have been the reasons for the selection of Parker as the preacher, it is plain that no one expected him to issue a manifesto of transcendentalist Unitarianism. Nor did Parker think of the occasion in such terms. His main thesis, indeed, was one that received the assent of a good many of the conservative Unitarians. He argued that certain elements in Christianity may be regarded as permanent and essential, while others are accidental and subject to transformation with the passing years. That which is permanent is the pure religion Jesus taught: "It is absolute, pure Morality; absolute, pure Religion; the love of man; the love of God acting without let or hindrance." Those things that are transient are the forms and doctrines with which Christianity has been clothed in successive periods of history. The rites that were regarded as essential in one age are abandoned by another; the heresy of one generation is the orthodoxy of the next. This transitoriness is the law of life; and who knows what absurdities future

generations will not find in forms and doctrines that we hold
dear? But if we are faithful, Parker declared, "the great truths
of morality and religion, the deep sentiment of love to man
and love to God, are perceived intuitively, and by instinct, as
it were, though our theology be imperfect and miserable."

If Parker had gone no further than this, the conservative
Unitarians might have questioned his reliance on intuition but
would not have become greatly exercised. The illustrations he
offered of the transitoriness of Christian doctrine, however,
touched two especially sensitive areas of theological debate.
In the first place, he suggested that the doctrine respecting the
origin and authority of the Bible has fluctuated widely. Over
long periods of time, the inspiration of its authors has been
declared to be infallible, despite the fact that it contains impossible legends, conflicting assertions in the record, and
imaginative stories which we shrink from accepting as literal
truth. But this idolatry of the Bible has not always existed; it
has no foundation in the book itself.

In the second place, Parker declared that opinions respecting the nature and authority of Christ have been constantly changing. With respect to his nature, scarcely two
Christian theologians have been fully agreed. To be sure, almost every sect has made Christianity to rest "on the personal
authority of Jesus, and not the immutable truth of the doctrines
themselves, or the authority of God, who sent him into the
world." But why should moral and religious truths depend on
the personal authority of their revealer, any more than scien-
tific truths depend on the personal authority of the investigator
who discovers them?

For opinions such as these, Parker was often described
as an "infidel" or a "deist." If one strips these terms of their
pejorative element, there is a sense in which they are not
inappropriate. In the usage of that day, both "infidelity" and
"deism" meant the denial that a specific, historical revelation
of God's will through Jesus Christ is absolutely essential for
the salvation of sinners. But it is important to recognize that
Parker was not a deist in the same sense that Paine and the
eighteenth-century freethinkers were. These men accepted the

sensational psychology of John Locke; and they believed in the sufficiency of natural religion, consisting of those doctrines which human reason can establish. Their attitude toward the Bible was often disrespectful, while their attitude toward Jesus ranged from genteel respect to outright scorn. Parker rejected the sensational psychology of Locke, so far as basic religious truths were concerned, and adhered to an intuitional philoso- ✓ phy. Hence he characteristically spoke of "absolute religion" instead of "natural religion." And while he rejected the infallibility of the Bible, he could say wholeheartedly: "How the truths of the Bible have blest us." While he refused to base Christian truth on the personal authority of Christ, his heart went out to Jesus with an almost evangelical warmth, as the Sermon itself bears witness.

The proceedings at the ordination went off uneventfully enough. One person rose during the sermon and walked out; but whether this was on account of "a badly ventilated building, or a heresy ventilated but too well," Parker's biographer did not presume to say.[41] Dr. Pierce's ordaining prayer was perhaps more pointed than it otherwise might have been in expressing "great reverence for the Holy Scriptures, for Jesus Christ, as the Mediator of the new covenant, sent to speak *with authority* to men."[42] After the service, Parker seems to have received the customary expressions of appreciation from those present, mingled with comments indicating qualified approval, at best, from some of his clerical brethren. No one, apparently, had the same sense of participation in a great occasion that had been so pervasive at the ordination of Sparks in Baltimore and at the valedictory exercises at the Divinity School. Certainly there was no hint of an impending controversy.

Whether the Unitarians, if left alone, would have made a public issue of the sermon may well be doubted. No comment on it appeared in the *Christian Register* until the orthodox party forced the issue, even though Samuel K. Lothrop,

[41] John Weiss, *Life and Correspondence of Theodore Parker* (New York, 1864), I, 170.
[42] *The South-Boston Unitarian Ordination* (Boston, 1841), p. 16.

one of the editors, had been a participant in the exercises. This discussion was precipitated by three clergymen who had been present, one a Congregationalist, another a Methodist, and the third a Baptist. They prepared a summary of Parker's discourse—at least the most offensive parts of it—as well as they could reconstruct it from memory and from notes taken at the time. This summary was then distributed for simultaneous publication in several orthodox religious journals. The purpose of the three ministers was not to argue against Parker; for it seemed to them that a mere statement of his doctrines would be enough to lay him open to condemnation. Their real hope was to smoke out the Unitarians and find out whether Parker would be disavowed by his fellow liberals. The orthodox had often declared that Unitarianism was only a halfway house to infidelity. Now they thought they saw an opportunity, if not to destroy Parker, at any rate to discredit the Unitarian body.

The Unitarians were in a decidely uncomfortable position. After all, Parker was in good ministerial standing with them, and most of them thought well of him. He was, admittedly, not always easy to live with; and in the years that followed, his sharp tongue did as much as his so-called infidelity to alienate many of his colleagues. But in 1841, he was generally liked and respected. Even when he made a characteristically tart response to an editorial in the *Register*, the editor's reply included expressions of the highest regard for Parker personally and praised both the purity of his character and his zealous devotion to the truth.

Furthermore, if the reaction of a minister like Samuel K. Lothrop is any indication, even conservative Unitarians agreed with most of what Parker had said. The passages that gave offense, Lothrop insisted, "though scattered throughout the discourse, might be compressed within the limits of a few of its pages." The main theme of the Sermon he accepted without hesitation. In parts of the discourse, Parker had illustrated his points "eloquently, justly and with power." Lothrop could only regret that elsewhere Parker had "made allusions and advanced thoughts and principles, which, if well founded, seem to us to overturn Christianity altogether, and at any rate, have made his sermon a firebrand in the community, rather than a word of peace, instruction and edification."[43]

The position of the Unitarians was made particularly difficult because they acknowledged the right and duty of all persons to search for truth, unfettered by creeds, confessions of faith, or other human standards of doctrine. During the Unitarian controversy a generation earlier, they had repeatedly insisted that the test of Christian fellowship must be Christian life and character, rather than doctrinal agreement. Now the orthodox were in a position to taunt the liberals and to inquire whether Christian fellowship was to mean fellowship with infidels and deists.

The Unitarians could not deny to Parker the right to speak his mind. But they did suggest that one who has reached conclusions that run counter to the established faith of the community must not be irresponsible in expression of them. In particular, an occasion must not be chosen when a preacher would inevitably be regarded as speaking for others and not simply stating personal views. This, indeed, was the great fault of both Emerson and Parker, that they chose ceremonial occasions, when the speaker customarily sought to express the consensus of the community, for a statement of views unacceptable to the group.

Parker's sermon "was not appropriate to the occasion," Lothrop complained. Such views, if put forth at all, "should never have been put forth in an associated service, when a man was acting with others, and to some extent for others." Parker should have reserved them for another time, when he "was acting, writing or speaking for himself and himself only." Lothrop refused to take any responsibility for what had been said, and denied that the orthodox could rightly hold him and his Unitarian colleagues responsible. He could only regret that he had found himself associated with Parker on an occasion "in which, while he uttered many good things and many beautiful things, that came home to our hearts, he also uttered many others that grossly outraged our feelings, or if he

[43] *Christian Register*, July 3, 1841.

chooses to call them so, our prejudices."[44]

Hence the real problem posed for the Unitarians by Parker's unconventional views was not whether they were true or false. Men like Samuel K. Lothrop, Chandler Robbins, and Nathaniel L. Frothingham knew exactly where they stood on the theological issues at stake. But they were genuinely in a quandary as to whether, or to what extent, one holding Parker's views was to be accepted as within the fellowship of Christian ministers. By what right, for example, should Parker expect to continue as a member of the Boston Association of Ministers? Could he properly be asked to withdraw? Was there any way for the Unitarians to dissociate themselves from him without resorting to the same "system of exclusion" of which they themselves had once been victims?

This matter came to a head at a meeting of the Boston Association of Ministers in January, 1843. At meetings as early as the previous September, the members had discussed Parker's *Discourse of Matters Pertaining to Religion*, which was just off the press; but they felt some delicacy about commenting on his views when he was not present to reply. At the same time, they hesitated to request him to attend a meeting at which he was fully entitled to be present without a special invitation, lest it look like a summons. But they suggested that he come and talk things over in a friendly way, and he responded.

There followed one of the most extraordinary episodes in the whole history of American Unitarianism. Dr. Frothingham, of the First Church, characterized Parker's book as "vehemently deistical" and declared that "he could have no ministerial intercourse" with its author, "though still he hoped to have a friendly and social intercourse." Others present complained that Parker had criticized them unfairly for their part in an ecclesiastical council, recently held to settle a controversy in the Hollis Street Church. In response to Frothingham, Parker asked to know the "precise quiddity" that must be added to his absolute religion to make it qualify as Christianity. The answer was obvious: miracles and the authority

[44] *Ibid.*, June 26, 1841.

of Christ. Someone then said: "It is plain we can't have ministerial intercourse with Mr. Parker: he denies the miracles."

Chandler Robbins finally came to the point: "Since Mr.
Parker finds the feeling in respect to him is so general, I think
it is his duty to withdraw from the Association." Parker replied
that he considered the principle of free inquiry to be at stake;
that theological uniformity had never previously been required; and that he had no intention of resigning. It then
became apparent that, while the members would have been
very much relieved if Parker had taken the hint and resigned,
they were not disposed to prescribe a doctrinal test for mem-
bership. Parker had been asked to withdraw; he had declined;
and there was no way to exclude him without abandoning the
principle of free inquiry. So several of the members said kind
things about Parker's sincerity; he burst into tears and left the
room, where Dr. Frothingham shook him cordially by the hand
and expressed the hope that he would come to see him soon;
and the closest the Unitarians ever came to a heresy trial
was over.[45]

Not that all that separated Parker from his colleagues
was at once forgotten. The theological differences were much
too apparent, and Parker's contentious spirit did nothing to
heal the breach. Ever since the South Boston Sermon, most
of the other Unitarian ministers had declined to exchange with
Parker, and they saw no reason to alter their course. Parker
was hurt by this form of ostracism but felt that he was not
entitled to complain. A ministerial exchange involved a personal relationship which might be freely offered but which, he
acknowledged, could no longer be claimed as a matter of right.

Perhaps the liberals had retreated a bit from the position
they had taken in the early years of the century, when the
orthodox had refused to exchange with them. Certainly his
colleagues' refusal seemed to Parker as clear an expression of
hostility as any formal vote of censure could have been. Yet,
by his refusal to withdraw from the Association when it would
have been all too easy to do so, Parker appealed successfully
to the consciences of his colleagues and forced them to reaf-

[45] Weiss, *Parker*, I, 188–93.

firm their loyalty to the principle of free inquiry. For while they felt no obligation to encourage or promote his wayward views, neither would they yield to the demand that "a rebuke be administered to him by some formal act of the denomination to which he has been considered as belonging." Ezra Stiles Gannett spoke their mind when he declared that such measures would be contrary to the spirit and practice of the denomination. The very fact, he suggested, "that for months the Unitarians have been urged from without and from within to denounce, or renounce, Mr. Parker, and yet have not found out how to do it, shows that it is strange work for them." It is not our way, he said, to pass votes of ecclesiastical censure. "We are willing . . . to take the principle of free inquiry with all its consequences."[46]

V

The historical significance of the three discourses here reprinted is clear. But they would not continue to be widely read were they of interest to historians only. What is it in them that later generations have found of lasting value? As Parker might have said: What is Transient and what Permanent in them?

Of the three discourses, the Baltimore Sermon was the one that was most specifically aimed at a particular theological situation. Necessarily, it seems somewhat dated. The principles of biblical criticism Channing advocated are still legitimate, but they have become commonplace. The kind of Calvinism against which he protested, with its somewhat mechanical and literal-minded understanding of the economy of redemption, no longer excites the imagination, and so polemics directed at it lose some of their original vitality. The versions of orthodox Christian doctrine that now attract attention, at least in theologically sophisticated circles, are much more likely to handle Christian theology in terms of mythology (in the best sense of the word), rather than as literal truth. Viewed in this way, Christian doctrine can be very subtle and appeal-

[46] Ezra Stiles Gannett, "Mr. Parker and his Views," *Christian Examiner*, XXXVIII (1845), 271, 272.

ing to the modern mind. But the Baltimore Sermon was too successful in meeting the issues of liberalism and orthodoxy in terms of the year 1819 to be very useful to liberals in the theological situation of today.

This does not mean that Channing himself is a figure of antiquarian or historical interest only. Actually, in the past two decades, more interest has been shown in Channing, both by historians and by philosophers, than in any comparable periods since the centennial celebrations of 1880. Far from being merely a shadowy figure of the past, he seems more alive and significant today than at any time in the past half-century. For a time, the renewed interest in his work focused on his role in shaping opinion on social issues, especially slavery; but recently his more strictly theological writings have been rediscovered. His openness to new ideas, his insistence that freedom is required for spiritual growth, and his confidence that human beings can make responsible use of intellectual and spiritual freedom are the themes of continuing significance in his work. These themes are not absent from the Baltimore Sermon, of course; but discourses such as "Likeness to God" (1828) and "Spiritual Freedom" (1830) give a quicker indication of where Channing's lasting influence lies.

The Divinity School Address was attacked because of its implications for a particular, temporary theological situation; but the special problem of miracles was really incidental to the main purpose of the discourse. Out of his immediate dissatisfaction with one particular minister, Emerson shaped his criticism of a perennial ecclesiastical situation. Formalism in religion was not peculiar to Emerson's day; and whenever the times call for a protest against overinstitutionalization or excessive deference to tradition in religion, Emerson's Address is available as an antidote. To be sure, our generation is much more likely to appreciate the values of the religious community than Emerson was; and so the historical judgment on churchmen like Andrews Norton or Henry Ware, Jr.—or even poor Barzillai Frost, who preached so badly but did his parish work so faithfully—is not so harsh as it once was. In short, we respond to Emerson's emphasis on spontaneity and

a direct relationship with the divine, especially because it is
presented with the magic of poetic language, even though we
know that spontaneity will not always sustain us, and prose
has its uses as well.

In an age like ours, sensitive as it is to all sorts of
relativities, we find it hard to accept Parker's concept of the
religious sentiment as the faculty by which we discern the
truths of Absolute Religion, or to regard the conscience as an
infallible and perfect moral guide. We are more likely to agree
with Channing when he declared—to Parker's amazement—
that the conscience must be educated. We tend to view with
suspicion the transcendentalist assertion of the primacy of
intuition in establishing religious and moral truth. A lot of
dangerous absolutisms, as well as Parker's benign Absolute
Religion, seem to lie that way.

Yet, while we have set aside this philosophy of intuition,
we have not abandoned a good many of the notions that the
Transcendentalists thought were rooted in it. Instead, we have
transplanted them to other soil, where they continue to have
life, even though the results would have surprised and even
troubled the Transcendentalists. This is notably true of Parker's distinction between the transient and the permanent in
Christianity. Parker assumed that there was such a thing as
Absolute Religion, of which the forms and doctrines of particular historical religions are but passing manifestations. The
religion of Jesus he identified with Absolute Religion, rather
than with transient forms and doctrines. To this extent, therefore, Parker considered Christianity to be in a separate category from other world religions, just as he thought of Jesus as
a religious leader of unique excellence. But what later generations have remembered is that Parker insisted that the Christianity of the churches is not necessarily true religion, and that
Christians are not the only ones who may have an instinctive
intuition of the divine.

Through the work of all three men, therefore, there runs
the assertion that we must not be content with inherited religious forms and doctrines, or satisfied with a traditional definition of our powers and potentialities. New light may still
break forth, and we are not now what we yet may be.

UNITARIAN CHRISTIANITY

By William Ellery Channing

Delivered at the Ordination of Rev. Jared Sparks in The First Independent Church of Baltimore on May 5, 1819.

> 1 THES. v. 21: "Prove all things; hold fast that which is good."

THE peculiar circumstances of this occasion not only justify, but seem to demand a departure from the course generally followed by preachers at the introduction of a brother into the sacred office. It is usual to speak of the nature, design, duties, and advantages of the Christian ministry; and on these topics I should now be happy to insist, did I not remember that a minister is to be given this day to a religious society, whose peculiarities of opinion have drawn upon them much remark, and may I not add, much reproach. Many good minds, many sincere Christians, I am aware, are apprehensive that the solemnities of this day are to give a degree of influence to principles which they deem false and injurious. The fears and anxieties of such men I respect; and, believing that they are grounded in part on mistake, I have thought it my duty to lay before you, as clearly as I can, some of the distinguishing opinions of that class of Christians in our country, who are known to sympathize with this religious society. I must ask your patience, for such a subject is not to be despatched in a narrow compass. I must also ask you to remember, that it is impossible to exhibit, in a single discourse, our views of every doctrine of Revelation, much less the differences of opinion which are known to subsist among ourselves. I shall confine myself to topics, on which our sentiments have been misrepresented, or which distinguish us most widely from others. May I not hope to be heard with candor? God deliver us all from prejudice and unkindness, and fill us with the love of truth and virtue.

There are two natural divisions under which my thoughts will be arranged. I shall endeavour to unfold, 1st, The principles which we adopt in interpreting the Scriptures. And 2dly, Some of the doctrines, which the Scriptures, so interpreted, seem to us clearly to express.

I. We regard the Scriptures as the records of God's successive revelations to mankind, and particularly of the last and most perfect revelation of his will by Jesus Christ. Whatever doctrines seem to us to be clearly taught in the Scriptures, we receive without reserve or exception. We do not, however, attach equal importance to all the books in this collection. Our religion, we believe, lies chiefly in the New Testament. The dispensation of Moses, compared with that of Jesus, we consider as adapted to the childhood of the human race, a preparation for a nobler system, and chiefly useful now as serving to confirm and illustrate the Christian Scriptures. Jesus Christ is the only master of Christians, and whatever he taught, either during his personal ministry, or by his inspired Apostles, we regard as of divine authority, and profess to make the rule of our lives.

This authority, which we give to the Scriptures, is a reason, we conceive, for studying them with peculiar care, and for inquiring anxiously into the principles of interpretation, by which their true meaning may be ascertained. The principles adopted by the class of Christians in whose name I speak, need to be explained, because they are often misunderstood. We are particularly accused of making an unwarrantable use of reason in the interpretation of Scripture. We are said to exalt reason above revelation, to prefer our own wisdom to God's. Loose and undefined charges of this kind are circulated so freely, that we think it due to ourselves, and to the cause of truth, to express our views with some particularity.

Our leading principle in interpreting Scripture is this, that the Bible is a book written for men, in the language of men, and that its meaning is to be sought in the same manner as that of other books. We believe that God, when he speaks to the human race, conforms, if we may so say, to the established rules of speaking and writing. How else would the Scriptures avail us more, than if communicated in an unknown tongue?

Now all books, and all conversation, require in the reader or hearer the constant exercise of reason; or their true import is only to be obtained by continual comparison and inference. Human language, you well know, admits various interpretations; and every word and every sentence must be modified and explained according to the subject which is discussed, according to the purposes, feelings, circumstances, and principles of the writer, and according to the genius and idioms of the language which he uses. These are acknowledged principles in the interpretation of human writings; and a man, whose words we should explain without reference to these principles, would reproach us justly with a criminal want of candor, and an intention of obscuring or distorting his meaning.

Were the Bible written in a language and style of its own, did it consist of words, which admit but a single sense, and of sentences wholly detached from each other, there would be no place for the principles now laid down. We could not reason about it, as about other writings. But such a book would be of little worth; and perhaps, of all books, the Scriptures correspond least to this description. The Word of God bears the stamp of the same hand, which we see in his works. It has infinite connexions and dependences. Every proposition is linked with others, and is to be compared with others; that its full and precise import may be understood. Nothing stands alone. The New Testament is built on the Old. The Christian dispensation is a continuation of the Jewish, the completion of a vast scheme of providence, requiring great extent of view in the reader. Still more, the Bible treats of subjects on which we receive ideas from other sources besides itself; such subjects as the nature, passions, relations, and duties of man; and it expects us to restrain and modify its language by the known truths, which observation and experience furnish on these topics.

We profess not to know a book, which demands a more frequent exercise of reason than the Bible. In addition to the remarks now made on its infinite connexions, we may observe, that its style nowhere affects the precision of science, or the accuracy of definition. Its language is singularly glowing, bold, and figurative, demanding more frequent departures from the literal sense, than that of our own age and country, and consequently demanding more continual exercise of judgment.—We find, too, that the different portions of this book, instead of being confined to general truths, refer perpetually to the times when they were written, to states of society, to modes of thinking, to controversies in the church, to feelings and usages which have passed away, and without the knowledge of which we are constantly in danger of extending to all times, and places, what was of temporary and local application.—We find, too, that some of these books are strongly marked by the genius and character of their respective writers, that the Holy Spirit did not so guide the Apostles as to suspend the peculiarities of their minds, and that a knowledge of their feelings, and of the influences under which they were placed, is one of the preparations for understanding their writings. With these views of the Bible, we feel it our bounden duty to exercise our reason upon it perpetually, to compare, to infer, to look beyond the letter to the spirit, to seek in the nature of the subject, and the aim of the writer, his true meaning; and, in general, to make use of what is known, for explaining what is difficult, and for discovering new truths.

Need I descend to particulars, to prove that the Scriptures demand the exercise of reason? Take, for example, the style in which they generally speak of God, and observe how habitually they apply to him human passions and organs. Recollect the declarations of Christ, that he came not to send peace, but a sword; that unless we eat his flesh, and drink his blood, we have no life in us; that we must hate father and mother, and pluck out the right eye; and a vast number of passages equally bold and unlimited. Recollect the unqualified manner in which it is said of Christians, that they possess all things, know all things, and can do all things. Recollect the verbal contradiction between Paul and James, and the apparent clashing of some parts of Paul's writings with the general doctrines and end of Christianity. I might extend the enumeration indefinitely; and who does not see, that we must limit all these passages by the known attributes of God, of Jesus Christ, and of human nature, and by the circumstances under which they were written, so as to give the language a quite different import from what it would require, had it been applied to different beings, or used in different connexions.

Enough has been said to show, in what sense we make use of reason in interpreting Scripture. From a variety of possible interpretations, we select that which accords with the nature of the subject and the state of the writer, with the connexion of the passage, with the general strain of Scripture, with the known character and will of God, and with the obvious and acknowledged laws of nature. In other words, we believe that God never contradicts, in one part of Scripture, what he teaches in another; and never contradicts, in revelation, what he teaches in his works and providence. And we therefore distrust every interpretation, which, after deliberate attention, seems repugnant to any established truth. We reason about the Bible precisely as civilians do about the constitution under which we live; who, you know, are accustomed to limit one provision of that venerable instrument by others, and to fix the precise import of its parts, by inquiring into its general spirit, into the intentions of its authors, and into the prevalent feelings, impressions, and circumstances of the time when it was framed. Without these principles of interpretation, we frankly acknowledge, that we cannot defend the divine authority of the Scriptures. Deny us this latitude, and we must abandon this book to its enemies.

We do not announce these principles as original, or

peculiar to ourselves. All Christians occasionally adopt them, not excepting those who most vehemently decry them, when they happen to menace some favorite article of their creed. All Christians are compelled to use them in their controversies with infidels. All sects employ them in their warfare with one another. All willingly avail themselves of reason, when it can be pressed into the service of their own party, and only complain of it, when its weapons wound themselves. None reason more frequently than those from whom we differ. It is astonishing what a fabric they rear from a few slight hints about the fall of our first parents; and how ingeniously they extract, from detached passages, mysterious doctrines about the divine nature. We do not blame them for reasoning so abundantly, but for violating the fundamental rules of reasoning, for sacrificing the plain to the obscure, and the general strain of Scripture to a scanty number of insulated texts.

We object strongly to the contemptuous manner in which human reason is often spoken of by our adversaries, because it leads, we believe, to universal skepticism. If reason be so dreadfully darkened by the fall, that its most decisive judgments on religion are unworthy of trust, then Christianity, and even natural theology, must be abandoned; for the existence and veracity of God, and the divine original of Christianity, are conclusions of reason, and must stand or fall with it. If revelation be at war with this faculty, it subverts itself, for the great question of its truth is left by God to be decided at the bar of reason. It is worthy of remark, how nearly the bigot and the skeptic approach. Both would annihilate our confidence in our faculties, and both throw doubt and confusion over every truth. We honor revelation too highly to make it the antagonist of reason, or to believe that it calls us to renounce our highest powers.

We indeed grant, that the use of reason in religion is accompanied with danger. But we ask any honest man to look back on the history of the church, and say, whether the renunciation of it be not still more dangerous. Besides, it is a plain fact, that men reason as erroneously on all subjects, as on religion. Who does not know the wild and groundless theories, which have been framed in physical and political science? But who ever supposed, that we must cease to exercise reason on nature and society, because men have erred for ages in explaining them? We grant, that the passions continually, and sometimes fatally, disturb the rational faculty in its inquiries into revelation. The ambitious contrive to find doctrines in the Bible, which favor their love of dominion. The timid and dejected discover there a gloomy system, and the mystical and fanatical, a visionary theology. The vicious can find examples or assertions on which to build the hope of a late repentance, or of acceptance on easy terms. The falsely refined contrive to light on doctrines which have not been soiled by vulgar handling. But the passions do not distract the reason in religious, any more than in other inquiries, which excite strong and general interest; and this faculty, of consequence, is not to be renounced in religion, unless we are prepared to discard it universally. The true inference from the almost endless errors, which have darkened theology, is, not that we are to neglect and disparage our powers, but to exert them more patiently, circumspectly, uprightly. The worst errors, after all, having sprung up in that church, which proscribes reason, and demands from its members implicit faith. The most pernicious doctrines have been the growth of the darkest times, when the general credulity encouraged bad men and enthusiasts to broach their dreams and inventions, and to stifle the faint remonstrances of reason, by the menaces of everlasting perdition. Say what we may, God has given us a rational nature, and will call us to account for it. We may let it sleep, but we do so at our peril. Revelation is addressed to us as rational beings. We may wish, in our sloth, that God had given us a system, demanding no labor of comparing, limiting, and inferring. But such a system would be at variance with the whole character of our present existence; and it is the part of wisdom to take revelation as it is given to us, and to interpret it by the help of the faculties, which it everywhere supposes, and on which it is founded.

To the views now given, an objection is commonly urged from the character of God. We are told, that God being infinitely wiser than men, his discoveries will surpass human reason. In a revelation from such a teacher, we ought to expect propositions, which we cannot reconcile with one another, and which may seem to contradict established truths; and it becomes us not to question or explain them away, but to believe, and adore, and to submit our weak and carnal reason to the Divine Word. To this objection, we have two short answers. We say, first, that it is impossible that a teacher of infinite wisdom should expose those, whom he would teach, to infinite error. But if once we admit, that propositions, which in their literal sense appear plainly repugnant to one another, or to any known truth, are still to be literally understood and received, what possible limit can we set to the belief of contradictions?

What shelter have we from the wildest fanaticism, which can always quote passages, that, in their literal and obvious sense, give support to its extravagances? How can the Protestant escape from transubstantiation, a doctrine most clearly taught us, if the submission of reason, now contended for, be a duty? How can we even hold fast the truth of revelation, for if one apparent contradiction may be true, so may another, and the proposition, that Christianity is false, though involving inconsistency, may still be a verity?

We answer again, that, if God be infinitely wise, he cannot sport with the understandings of his creatures. A wise teacher discovers his wisdom in adapting himself to the capacities of his pupils, not in perplexing them with what is unintelligible, not in distressing them with apparent contradictions, not in filling them with a skeptical distrust of their own powers. An infinitely wise teacher, who knows the precise extent of our minds, and the best method of enlightening them, will surpass all other instructors in bringing down truth to our apprehension, and in showing its loveliness and harmony. We ought, indeed, to expect occasional obscurity in such a book as the Bible, which was written for past and future ages, as well as for the present. But God's wisdom is a pledge, that whatever is necessary for *us,* and necessary for salvation, is revealed too plainly to be mistaken, and too consistently to be questioned, by a sound and upright mind. It is not the mark of wisdom, to use an unintelligible phraseology, to communicate what is above our capacities, to confuse and unsettle the intellect by appearances of contradiction. We honor our Heavenly Teacher too much to ascribe to him such a revelation. A revelation is a gift of light. It cannot thicken our darkness, and multiply our perplexities.

II. Having thus stated the principles according to which we interpret Scripture, I now proceed to the second great head of this discourse, which is, to state some of the views which we derive from that sacred book, particularly those which distinguish us from other Christians.

1. In the first place, we believe in the doctrine of God's UNITY, or that there is one God, and one only. To this truth we give infinite importance, and we feel ourselves bound to take heed, lest any man spoil us of it by vain philosophy. The proposition, that there is one God, seems to us exceedingly plain. We understand by it, that there is one being, one mind, one person, one intelligent agent, and one only, to whom underived and infinite perfection and dominion belong. We conceive, that these words could have conveyed no other meaning to the simple and uncultivated people who were set apart to be the depositaries of this great truth, and who were utterly incapable of understanding those hairbreadth distinctions between being and person, which the sagacity of later ages has discovered. We find no intimation, that this language was to be taken in an unusual sense, or that God's unity was a quite different thing from the oneness of other intelligent beings.

We object to the doctrine of the Trinity, that, whilst acknowledging in words, it subverts in effect, the unity of God. According to this doctrine, there are three infinite and equal persons, possessing supreme divinity, called the Father, Son, and Holy Ghost. Each of these persons, as described by theologians, has his own particular consciousness, will, and perceptions. They love each other, converse with each other, and delight in each other's society. They perform different parts in man's redemption, each having his appropriate office, and neither doing the work of the other.

The Son is mediator and not the Father. The Father sends
the Son, and is not himself sent; nor is he conscious, like the
Son, of taking flesh. Here, then, we have three intelligent
agents, possessed of different consciousnesses, different wills,
and different perceptions, performing different acts, and
sustaining different relations; and if these things do not imply
and constitute three minds or beings, we are utterly at a loss
to know how three minds or beings are to be formed. It is
difference of properties, and acts, and consciousness, which
leads us to the belief of different intelligent beings, and, if
this mark fails us, our whole knowledge fall ; we have no
proof, that all the agents and persons in the uı iverse are not
one and the same mind. When we attempt to conceive of
three Gods, we can do nothing more than represent to ourselves three agents, distinguished from each other by similar
marks and peculiarities to those which separate the persons
of the Trinity; and when common Christians hear these persons spoken of as conversing with each other, loving each
other, and performing different acts, how can they help re-
garding them as different beings, different minds?

We do, then, with all earnestness, though without re-
proaching our brethren, protest against the irrational and
unscriptural doctrine of the Trinity. "To us," as to the
Apostle and the primitive Christians, "there is one God,
even the Father." With Jesus, we worship the Father, as the
only living and true God. We are astonished, that any man
can read the New Testament, and avoid the conviction, that
the Father alone is God. We hear our Saviour continually
appropriating this character to the Father. We find the Father continually distinguished from Jesus by this title. "God
sent his Son." "God anointed Jesus." Now, how singular
and inexplicable is this phraseology, which fills the New

Testament, if this title belong equally to Jesus, and if a principal object of this book is to reveal him as God, as partaking equally with the Father in supreme divinity! We challenge our opponents to adduce one passage in the New Testament, where the word God means three persons, where it is not limited to one person, and where, unless turned from its usual sense by the connexion, it does not mean the Father. Can stronger proof be given, that the doctrine of three persons in the Godhead is not a fundamental doctrine of Christianity?

This doctrine, were it true, must, from its difficulty, singularity, and importance, have been laid down with great clearness, guarded with great care, and stated with all possible precision. But where does this statement appear? From the many passages which treat of God, we ask for one, one only, in which we are told, that he is a threefold being, or that he is three persons, or that he is Father, Son, and Holy Ghost. On the contrary, in the New Testament, where, at least, we might expect many express assertions of this nature, God is declared to be one, without the least attempt to prevent the acceptation of the words in their common sense; and he is always spoken of and addressed in the singular number, that is, in language which was universally understood to intend a single person, and to which no other idea could have been attached, without an express admonition. So entirely do the Scriptures abstain from stating the Trinity, that when our opponents would insert it into their creeds and doxologies, they are compelled to leave the Bible, and to invent forms of words altogether unsanctioned by Scriptural phraseology. That a doctrine so strange, so liable to misapprehension, so fundamental as this is said to be, and requiring such careful exposition, should be left so undefined and unprotected, to be made out by inference, and to be hunted through distant and detached parts of Scripture, this is a difficulty, which, we think, no ingenuity can explain.

We have another difficulty. Christianity, it must be remembered, was planted and grew up amidst sharp-sighted enemies, who overlooked no objectionable part of the system, and who must have fastened with great earnestness on a doctrine involving such apparent contradictions as the Trinity. We cannot conceive an opinion, against which the Jews, who prided themselves on an adherence to God's unity, would have raised an equal clamor. Now, how happens it, that in the apostolic writings, which relate so much to objections against Christianity, and to the controversies which grew out of this religion, not one word is said, implying that objections were brought against the Gospel from the doctrine of the Trinity, not one word is uttered in its defence and explanation, not a word to rescue it from reproach and mistake? This argument has almost the force of demonstration. We are persuaded, that had three divine persons been announced by the first preachers of Christianity, all equal, and all infinite, one of whom was the very Jesus who had lately died on a cross, this peculiarity of Christianity would have almost absorbed every other, and the great labor of the Apostles would have been to repel the continual assaults, which it would have awakened. But the fact is, that not a whisper of objection to Christianity, on that account, reaches our ears from the apostolic age. In the Epistles we see not a trace of controversy called forth by the Trinity.

We have further objections to this doctrine, drawn from its practical influence. We regard it as unfavorable to devotion, by dividing and distracting the mind in its com-

munion with God. It is a great excellence of the doctrine of
God's unity, that it offers to us ONE OBJECT of supreme
homage, adoration, and love, One Infinite Father, one Being
of beings, one original and fountain, to whom we may refer
all good, in whom all our powers and affections may be concentrated, and whose lovely and venerable nature may pervade all our thoughts. True piety, when directed to an un-
divided Deity, has a chasteness, a singleness, most favorable
to religious awe and love. Now, the Trinity sets before us
three distinct objects of supreme adoration; three infinite
persons, having equal claims on our hearts; three divine
agents, performing different offices, and to be acknowledged
and worshipped in different relations. And is it possible, we
ask, that the weak and limited mind of man can attach itself
to these with the same power and joy, as to One Infinite
Father, the only First Cause, in whom all the blessings of
nature and redemption meet as their centre and source?
Must not devotion be distracted by the equal and rival claims
of three equal persons, and must not the worship of the con-
scientious, consistent Christian, be disturbed by an apprehension, lest he withhold from one or another of these, his
due proportion of homage?

We also think, that the doctrine of the Trinity injures
devotion, not only by joining to the Father other objects of
worship, but by taking from the Father the supreme affection, which is his due, and transferring it to the Son. This
is a most important view. That Jesus Christ, if exalted into
the infinite Divinity, should be more interesting than the
Father, is precisely what might be expected from history,
and from the principles of human nature. Men want an
object of worship like themselves, and the great secret of
idolatry lies in this propensity. A God, clothed in our form,

and feeling our wants and sorrows, speaks to our weak nature more strongly, than a Father in heaven, a pure spirit, invisible and unapproachable, save by the reflecting and purified mind.—We think, too, that the peculiar offices ascribed to Jesus by the popular theology, make him the most attractive person in the Godhead. The Father is the depositary of the justice, the vindicator of the rights, the avenger of the laws of the Divinity. On the other hand, the Son, the brightness of the divine mercy, stands between the incensed Deity and guilty humanity, exposes his meek head to the storms, and his compassionate breast to the sword of the divine justice, bears our whole load of punishment, and purchases with his blood every blessing which descends from heaven. Need we state the effect of these representations, especially on common minds, for whom Christianity was chiefly designed, and whom it seeks to bring to the Father as the loveliest being? We do believe, that the worship of a bleeding, suffering God, tends strongly to absorb the mind, and to draw it from other objects, just as the human tenderness of the Virgin Mary has given her so conspicuous a place in the devotions of the Church of Rome. We believe, too, that this worship, though attractive, is not most fitted to spiritualize the mind, that it awakens human transport, rather than that deep veneration of the moral perfections of God, which is the essence of piety.

2. Having thus given our views of the unity of God, I proceed in the second place to observe, that we believe in the unity of Jesus Christ. We believe that Jesus is one mind, one soul, one being, as truly one as we are, and equally distinct from the one God. We complain of the doctrine of the Trinity, that, not satisfied with making God three beings, it makes Jesus Christ two beings, and thus introduces infinite

confusion into our conceptions of his character. This corruption of Christianity, alike repugnant to common sense and to the general strain of Scripture, is a remarkable proof of the power of a false philosophy in disfiguring the simple truth of Jesus.

According to this doctrine, Jesus Christ, instead of being one mind, one conscious intelligent principle, whom we can understand, consists of two souls, two minds; the one divine, the other human; the one weak, the other almighty; the one ignorant, the other omniscient. Now we maintain, that this is to make Christ two beings. To denominate him one person, one being, and yet to suppose him made up of two minds, infinitely different from each other, is to abuse and confound language, and to throw darkness over all our conceptions of intelligent natures. According to the common doctrine, each of these two minds in Christ has its own consciousness, its own will, its own perceptions. They have, in fact, no common properties. The divine mind feels none of the wants and sorrows of the human, and the human is infinitely removed from the perfection and happiness of the divine. Can you conceive of two beings in the universe more distinct? We have always thought that one person was constituted and distinguished by one consciousness. The doctrine, that one and the same person should have two consciousnesses, two wills, two souls, infinitely different from each other, this we think an enormous tax on human credulity.

We say, that if a doctrine, so strange, so difficult, so remote from all the previous conceptions of men, be indeed a part and an essential part of revelation, it must be taught with great distinctness, and we ask our brethren to point to some plain, direct passage, where Christ is said to be composed of two minds infinitely different, yet constituting one person. We find none. Other Christians, indeed, tell us, that this doctrine is necessary to the harmony of the Scriptures, that some texts ascribe to Jesus Christ human, and others divine properties, and that to reconcile these, we must suppose two minds, to which these properties may be referred. In other words, for the purpose of reconciling certain difficult passages, which a just criticism can in a great degree, if not wholly, explain, we must invent an hypothesis vastly more difficult, and involving gross absurdity. We are to find our way out of a labyrinth, by a clue which conducts us into mazes infinitely more inextricable.

Surely, if Jesus Christ felt that he consisted of two minds, and that this was a leading feature of his religion, his phraseology respecting himself would have been colored by this peculiarity. The universal language of men is framed upon the idea, that one person is one person, is one mind, and one soul; and when the multitude heard this language from the lips of Jesus, they must have taken it in its usual sense, and must have referred to a single soul all which he spoke, unless expressly instructed to interpret it differently. But where do we find this instruction? Where do you meet, in the New Testament, the phraseology which abounds in Trinitarian books, and which necessarily grows from the doctrine of two natures in Jesus? Where does this divine teacher say, "This I speak as God, and this as man; this is true only of my human mind, this only of my divine"? Where do we find in the Epistles a trace of this strange phraseology? Nowhere. It was not needed in that day. It was demanded by the errors of a later age.

We believe, then, that Christ is one mind, one being, and, I add, a being distinct from the one God. That Christ

is not the one God, not the same being with the Father, is a
necessary inference from our former head, in which we saw
that the doctrine of three persons in God is a fiction. But
on so important a subject, I would add a few remarks. We
wish, that those from whom we differ, would weigh one
striking fact. Jesus, in his preaching, continually spoke of
God. The word was always in his mouth. We ask, does he,
by this word, ever mean himself? We say, never. On the
contrary, he most plainly distinguishes between God and
himself, and so do his disciples. How this is to be reconciled
with the idea, that the manifestation of Christ, as God, was
a primary object of Christianity, our adversaries must determine.

If we examine the passages in which Jesus is distinguished from God, we shall see, that they not only speak of
him as another being, but seem to labor to express his inferiority. He is continually spoken of as the Son of God, sent
of God, receiving all his powers from God, working miracles
because God was with him, judging justly because God
taught him, having claims on our belief, because he was
anointed and sealed by God, and as able of himself to do
nothing. The New Testament is filled with this language.
Now we ask, what impression this language was fitted and
intended to make? Could any, who heard it, have imagined
that Jesus was the very God to whom he was so industriously
declared to be inferior; the very Being by whom he was sent,
and from whom he professed to have received his message
and power? Let it here be remembered, that the human
birth, and bodily form, and humble circumstances, and
mortal sufferings of Jesus, must all have prepared men to
interpret, in the most unqualified manner, the language in
which his inferiority to God was declared. Why, then, was

this language used so continually, and without limitation, if Jesus were the Supreme Deity, and if this truth were an essential part of his religion? I repeat it, the human condition and sufferings of Christ tended strongly to exclude from men's minds the idea of his proper Godhead; and, of course, we should expect to find in the New Testament perpetual care and effort to counteract this tendency, to hold him forth as the same being with his Father, if this doctrine were, as is pretended, the soul and centre of his religion. We should expect to find the phraseology of Scripture cast into the mould of this doctrine, to hear familiarly of God the Son, of our Lord God Jesus, and to be told, that to us there is one God, even Jesus. But, instead of this, the inferiority of Christ pervades the New Testament. It is not only implied in the general phraseology, but repeatedly and decidedly expressed, and unaccompanied with any admonition to prevent its application to his whole nature. Could it, then, have been the great design of the sacred writers to exhibit Jesus as the Supreme God?

I am aware that these remarks will be met by two or three texts, in which Christ is called God, and by a class of passages, not very numerous, in which divine properties are said to be ascribed to him. To these we offer one plain answer. We say, that it is one of the most established and obvious principles of criticism, that language is to be explained according to the known properties of the subject to which it is applied. Every man knows, that the same words convey very different ideas, when used in relation to different beings. Thus, Solomon *built* the temple in a different manner from the architect whom he employed; and God *repents* differently from man. Now we maintain, that the known properties and circumstances of Christ, his birth, sufferings, and death, his constant habit of speaking of God as a distinct being from himself, his praying to God, his ascribing to God all his power and offices, these acknowledged properties of Christ, we say, oblige us to interpret the comparatively few passages which are thought to make him the Supreme God, in a manner consistent with his distinct and inferior nature. It is our duty to explain such texts by the rule which we apply to other texts, in which human beings are called gods, and are said to be partakers of the divine nature, to know and possess all things, and to be filled with all God's fulness. These latter passages we do not hesitate to modify, and restrain, and turn from the most obvious sense, because this sense is opposed to the known properties of the beings to whom they relate; and we maintain, that we adhere to the same principle, and use no greater latitude, in explaining, as we do, the passages which are thought to support the Godhead of Christ.

Trinitarians profess to derive some important advantages from their mode of viewing Christ. It furnishes them, they tell us, with an infinite atonement, for it shows them an infinite being suffering for their sins. The confidence with which this fallacy is repeated astonishes us. When pressed with the question, whether they really believe, that the infinite and unchangeable God suffered and died on the cross, they acknowledge that this is not true, but that Christ's human mind alone sustained the pains of death. How have we, then, an infinite sufferer? This language seems to us an imposition on common minds, and very derogatory to God's justice, as if this attribute could be satisfied by a sophism and a fiction.

We are also told, that Christ is a more interesting object, that his love and mercy are more felt, when he is viewed as the Supreme God, who left his glory to take humanity and to suffer for men. That Trinitarians are strongly moved by this representation, we do not mean to deny; but we think their emotions altogether founded on a misapprehension of their own doctrines. They talk of the second person of the Trinity's leaving his glory and his Father's bosom, to visit and save the world. But this second person, being the unchangeable and infinite God, was evidently incapable of parting with the least degree of his perfection and felicity. At the moment of his taking flesh, he was as intimately present with his Father as before, and equally with his Father filled heaven, and earth, and immensity. This Trinitarians acknowledge; and still they profess to be touched and overwhelmed by the amazing humiliation of this immutable being! But not only does their doctrine, when fully explained, reduce Christ's humiliation to a fiction, it almost wholly destroys the impressions with which his cross ought to be viewed. According to their doctrine, Christ was comparatively no sufferer at all. It is true, his human mind suffered; but this, they tell us, was an infinitely small part of Jesus, bearing no more proportion to his whole nature, than a single hair of our heads to the whole body, or than a drop to the ocean. The divine mind of Christ, that which was most properly himself, was infinitely happy, at the very moment of the suffering of his humanity. Whilst hanging on the cross, he was the happiest being in the universe, as happy as the infinite Father; so that his pains, compared with his felicity, were nothing. This Trinitarians do, and must, acknowledge. It follows necessarily from the immutableness of the divine nature, which they ascribe to Christ; so that their system, justly viewed, robs his death of interest, weakens our sympathy with his sufferings, and is, of all others, most unfavorable to a love of Christ, founded on a sense of his sacrifices for mankind. We esteem our own views to be vastly more affecting. It is our belief, that Christ's humiliation was real and entire, that the whole Saviour, and not a part of him, suffered, that his crucifixion was a scene of deep and unmixed agony. As we stand round his cross, our minds are not distracted, nor our sensibility weakened, by contemplating him as composed of incongruous and infinitely differing minds, and as having a balance of infinite felicity. We recognise in the dying Jesus but one mind. This, we think, renders his sufferings, and his patience and love in bearing them, incomparably more impressive and affecting than the system we oppose.

3. Having thus given our belief on two great points, namely, that there is one God, and that Jesus Christ is a being distinct from, and inferior to, God, I now proceed to another point, on which we lay still greater stress. We believe in the *moral perfection of God*. We consider no part of theology so important as that which treats of God's moral character; and we value our views of Christianity chiefly as they assert his amiable and venerable attributes.

It may be said, that, in regard to this subject, all Christians agree, that all ascribe to the Supreme Being infinite justice, goodness, and holiness. We reply, that it is very possible to speak of God magnificently, and to think of him meanly; to apply to his person high-sounding epithets, and to his government, principles which make him odious. The Heathens called Jupiter the greatest and the best; but his history was black with cruelty and lust. We cannot judge of men's real ideas of God by their general language, for in all ages they have hoped to soothe the Deity by adulation. We must inquire into their particular views of his purposes, of the principles of his administration, and of his disposition towards his creatures.

We conceive that Christians have generally leaned towards a very injurious view of the Supreme Being. They have too often felt, as if he were raised, by his greatness and sovereignty, above the principles of morality, above those eternal laws of equity and rectitude, to which all other beings are subjected. We believe, that in no being is the sense of right so strong, so omnipotent, as in God. We believe that his almighty power is entirely submitted to his perceptions of rectitude; and this is the ground of our piety. It is not because he is our Creator merely, but because he created us for good and holy purposes; it is not because his will is irresistible, but because his will is the perfection of virtue, that we pay him allegiance. We cannot bow before a being, however great and powerful, who governs tyrannically. We respect nothing but excellence, whether on earth or in heaven. We venerate not the loftiness of God's throne, but the equity and goodness in which it is established.

We believe that God is infinitely good, kind, benevolent, in the proper sense of these words; good in disposition, as well as in act; good, not to a few, but to all; good to every individual, as well as to the general system.

We believe, too, that God is just; but we never forget, that his justice is the justice of a good being, dwelling in the same mind, and acting in harmony, with perfect benevolence. By this attribute, we understand God's infinite regard to virtue or moral worth, expressed in a moral government; that is, in giving excellent and equitable laws, and in conferring such rewards, and inflicting such punishments, as are best fitted to secure their observance. God's justice has for its end the highest virtue of the creation, and it punishes for this end alone, and thus it coincides with benevolence; for virtue and happiness, though not the same, are inseparably conjoined.

God's justice thus viewed, appears to us to be in perfect harmony with his mercy. According to the prevalent systems of theology, these attributes are so discordant and jarring, that to reconcile them is the hardest task, and the most wonderful achievement, of infinite wisdom. To us they seem to be intimate friends, always at peace, breathing the same spirit, and seeking the same end. By God's mercy, we understand not a blind instinctive compassion, which forgives without reflection, and without regard to the interests of virtue. This, we acknowledge, would be incompatible with justice, and also with enlightened benevolence. God's mercy, as we understand it, desires strongly the happiness of the guilty, but only through their penitence. It has a regard to character as truly as his justice. It defers punishment, and suffers long, that the sinner may return to his duty, but leaves the impenitent and unyielding, to the fearful retribution threatened in God's Word.

To give our views of God in one word, we believe in his Parental character. We ascribe to him, not only the name, but the dispositions and principles of a father. We believe that he has a father's concern for his creatures, a father's desire for their improvement, a father's equity in proportioning his commands to their powers, a father's joy in their progress, a father's readiness to receive the penitent, and a father's justice for the incorrigible. We look upon this world as a place of education, in which he is training men by prosperity and adversity, by aids and obstructions, by conflicts of reason and passion, by motives to duty and temptations to sin, by a various discipline suited to free and moral beings, for union with himself, and for a sublime and ever-growing virtue in heaven.

Now, we object to the systems of religion, which prevail among us, that they are adverse, in a greater or less degree, to these purifying, comforting, and honorable views of God; that they take from us our Father in heaven, and substitute for him a being, whom we cannot love if we would, and whom we ought not to love if we could. We object, particularly on this ground, to that system, which arrogates to itself the name of Orthodoxy, and which is now industriously propagated through our country. This system indeed takes various shapes, but in all it casts dishonor on the Creator. According to its old and genuine form, it teaches, that God brings us into life wholly depraved, so that under the innocent features of our childhood is hidden a nature averse to all good and propense to all evil, a nature which exposes us to God's displeasure and wrath, even before we have acquired power to understand our duties, or to reflect upon our actions. According to a more modern exposition, it teaches, that we came from the hands of our Maker with such a constitution, and are placed under such influences and circumstances, as to render certain and infallible the total depravity of every human being, from the first moment of his moral agency; and it also teaches, that the offence of the child, who brings into life this ceaseless tendency to unmingled crime, exposes him to the sentence of everlasting damnation. Now, according to the plainest principles of morality, we maintain, that a natural constitution of the mind, unfailingly disposing it to evil and to evil alone, would absolve it from guilt; that to give existence under this condition would argue unspeakable cruelty; and that to

punish the sin of this unhappily constituted child with endless ruin, would be a wrong unparalleled by the most merci-
less despotism.

This system also teaches, that God selects from this
corrupt mass a number to be saved, and plucks them, by a
special influence, from the common ruin; that the rest of
mankind, though left without that special grace which their
conversion requires, are commanded to repent, under penalty of aggravated woe; and that forgiveness is promised
them, on terms which their very constitution infallibly dis-
poses them to reject, and in rejecting which they awfully
enhance the punishments of hell. These proffers of forgiveness and exhortations of amendment, to beings born under
a blighting curse, fill our minds with a horror which we want
words to express.

That this religious system does not produce all the
effects on character, which might be anticipated, we most
joyfully admit. It is often, very often, counteracted by
nature, conscience, common sense, by the general strain of
Scripture, by the mild example and precepts of Christ, and
by the many positive declarations of God's universal kindness and perfect equity. But still we think that we see its
unhappy influence. It tends to discourage the timid, to give
excuses to the bad, to feed the vanity of the fanatical, and to
offer shelter to the bad feelings of the malignant. By shock-
ing, as it does, the fundamental principles of morality, and
by exhibiting a severe and partial Deity, it tends strongly to
pervert the moral faculty, to form a gloomy, forbidding, and
servile religion, and to lead men to substitute censoriousness,
bitterness, and persecution, for a tender and impartial charity. We think, too, that this system, which begins with degrading human nature, may be expected to end in pride;

for pride grows out of a consciousness of high distinctions, however obtained, and no distinction is so great as that which is made between the elected and abandoned of God.

The false and dishonorable views of God, which have now been stated, we feel ourselves bound to resist unceasingly. Other errors we can pass over with comparative indifference. But we ask our opponents to leave to us a GOD, worthy of our love and trust, in whom our moral sentiments may delight, in whom our weaknesses and sorrows may find refuge. We cling to the Divine perfections. We meet them everywhere in creation, we read them in the Scriptures, we see a lovely image of them in Jesus Christ; and gratitude, love, and veneration call on us to assert them. Reproached, as we often are, by men, it is our consolation and happiness, that one of our chief offences is the zeal with which we vindicate the dishonored goodness and rectitude of God.

4. Having thus spoken of the unity of God; of the unity of Jesus, and his inferiority to God; and of the perfections of the Divine character; I now proceed to give our views of the mediation of Christ, and of the purposes of his mission. With regard to the great object which Jesus came to accomplish, there seems to be no possibility of mistake. We believe, that he was sent by the Father to effect a moral, or spiritual deliverance of mankind; that is, to rescue men from sin and its consequences, and to bring them to a state of everlasting purity and happiness. We believe, too, that he accomplishes this sublime purpose by a variety of methods; by his instructions respecting God's unity, parental character, and moral government, which are admirably fitted to reclaim the world from idolatry and impiety, to the knowledge, love, and obedience of the Creator; by his promises of pardon to the penitent, and of divine assistance to those who labor for

progress in moral excellence; by the light which he has thrown on the path of duty; by his own spotless example, in which the loveliness and sublimity of virtue shine forth to warm and quicken, as well as guide us to perfection; by his threatenings against incorrigible guilt; by his glorious discoveries of immortality; by his sufferings and death; by that signal event, the resurrection, which powerfully bore witness to his divine mission, and brought down to men's senses a future life; by his continual intercession, which obtains for us spiritual aid and blessings; and by the power with which he is invested of raising the dead, judging the world, and conferring the everlasting rewards promised to the faithful.

We have no desire to conceal the fact, that a difference of opinion exists among us, in regard to an interesting part of Christ's mediation; I mean, in regard to the precise influence of his death on our forgiveness. Many suppose, that this event contributes to our pardon, as it was a principal means of confirming his religion, and of giving it a power over the mind; in other words, that it procures forgiveness by leading to that repentance and virtue, which is the great and only condition on which forgiveness is bestowed. Many of us are dissatisfied with this explanation, and think that the Scriptures ascribe the remission of sins to Christ's death, with an emphasis so peculiar, that we ought to consider this event as having a special influence in removing punishment, though the Scriptures may not reveal the way in which it contributes to this end.

Whilst, however, we differ in explaining the connexion between Christ's death and human forgiveness, a connexion which we all gratefully acknowledge, we agree in rejecting many sentiments which prevail in regard to his mediation. The idea, which is conveyed to common minds by the pop-

ular system, that Christ's death has an influence in making
God placable, or merciful, in awakening his kindness towards men, we reject with strong disapprobation. We are
happy to find, that this very dishonorable notion is disowned
by intelligent Christians of that class from which we differ.
We recollect, however, that, not long ago, it was common
to hear of Christ, as having died to appease God's wrath,
and to pay the debt of sinners to his inflexible justice; and
we have a strong persuasion, that the language of popular
religious books, and the common mode of stating the doctrine of Christ's mediation, still communicate very degrading views of God's character. They give to multitudes the
impression, that the death of Jesus produces a change in the
mind of God towards man, and that in this its efficacy chiefly
consists. No error seems to us more pernicious. We can endure no shade over the pure goodness of God. We earnestly
maintain, that Jesus, instead of calling forth, in any way or
degree, the mercy of the Father, was sent by that mercy, to
be our Saviour; that he is nothing to the human race, but
what he is by God's appointment; that he communicates
nothing but what God empowers him to bestow; that our
Father in heaven is originally, essentially, and eternally
placable, and disposed to forgive; and that his unborrowed,
underived, and unchangeable love is the only fountain of
what flows to us through his Son. We conceive, that Jesus
is dishonored, not glorified, by ascribing to him an influence,
which clouds the splendor of Divine benevolence.

We farther agree in rejecting, as unscriptural and absurd, the explanation given by the popular system, of the
manner in which Christ's death procures forgiveness for
men. This system used to teach as its fundamental principle, that man, having sinned against an infinite Being, has

contracted infinite guilt, and is consequently exposed to an infinite penalty. We believe, however, that this reasoning, if reasoning it may be called, which overlooks the obvious maxim, that the guilt of a being must be proportioned to his nature and powers, has fallen into disuse. Still the system teaches, that sin, of whatever degree, exposes to endless punishment, and that the whole human race, being infallibly involved by their nature in sin, owe this awful penalty to the justice of their Creator. It teaches, that this penalty cannot be remitted, in consistency with the honor of the divine law, unless a substitute be found to endure it or to suffer an equivalent. It also teaches, that, from the nature of the case, no substitute is adequate to this work, save the infinite God himself; and accordingly, God, in his second person, took on him human nature, that he might pay to his own justice the debt of punishment incurred by men, and might thus reconcile forgiveness with the claims and threatenings of his law. Such is the prevalent system. Now, to us, this doctrine seems to carry on its front strong marks of absurdity; and we maintain that Christianity ought not to be encumbered with it, unless it be laid down in the New Testament fully and expressly. We ask our adversaries, then, to point to some plain passages where it is taught. We ask for one text, in which we are told, that God took human nature that he might make an infinite satisfaction to his own justice; for one text, which tells us, that human guilt requires an infinite substitute; that Christ's sufferings owe their efficacy to their being borne by an infinite being; or that his divine nature gives infinite value to the sufferings of the human. Not *one word* of this description can we find in the Scriptures; not a text, which even hints at these strange doctrines. They are altogether, we believe, the fictions of theologians. Christianity is in no degree responsible for them. We are astonished at their prevalence. What can be plainer, than that God cannot, in any sense, be a sufferer, or bear a penalty in the room of his creatures? How dishonorable to him is the supposition, that his justice is now so severe, as to exact infinite punishment for the sins of frail and feeble men, and now so easy and yielding, as to accept the limited pains of Christ's human soul, as a full equivalent for the endless woes due from the world? How plain is it also, according to this doctrine, that God, instead of being plenteous in forgiveness, never forgives; for it seems absurd to speak of men as forgiven, when their whole punishment, or an equivalent to it, is borne by a substitute? A scheme more fitted to obscure the brightness of Christianity and the mercy of God, or less suited to give comfort to a guilty and troubled mind, could not, we think, be easily framed.

We believe, too, that this system is unfavorable to the character. It naturally leads men to think, that Christ came to change God's mind rather than their own; that the highest object of his mission was to avert punishment, rather than to communicate holiness; and that a large part of religion consists in disparaging good works and human virtue, for the purpose of magnifying the value of Christ's vicarious sufferings. In this way, a sense of the infinite importance and indispensable necessity of personal improvement is weakened, and high-sounding praises of Christ's cross seem often to be substituted for obedience to his precepts. For ourselves, we have not so learned Jesus. Whilst we gratefully acknowledge, that he came to rescue us from punishment, we believe, that he was sent on a still nobler errand, namely, to deliver us from sin itself, and to form us to a sublime and heavenly virtue. We regard him as a Saviour, chiefly as he is the light, physician, and guide of the dark, diseased, and wandering mind. No influence in the universe seems to us so glorious, as that over the character; and no redemption so worthy of thankfulness, as the restoration of the soul to purity. Without this, pardon, were it possible, would be of little value. Why pluck the sinner from hell, if a hell be left to burn in his own breast? Why raise him to heaven, if he remain a stranger to its sanctity and love? With these impressions, we are accustomed to value the Gospel chiefly as it abounds in effectual aids, motives, excitements to a generous and divine virtue. In this virtue, as in a common centre, we see all its doctrines, precepts, promises meet; and we believe, that faith in this religion is of no worth, and contributes nothing to salvation, any farther than as it uses these doctrines, precepts, promises, and the whole life, character, sufferings, and triumphs of Jesus, as the means of purifying the mind, of changing it into the likeness of his celestial excellence.

5. Having thus stated our views of the highest object of Christ's mission, that it is the recovery of men to virtue, or holiness, I shall now, in the last place, give our views of the nature of Christian virtue, or true holiness. We believe that all virtue has its foundation in the moral nature of man, that is, in conscience, or his sense of duty, and in the power of forming his temper and life according to conscience. We believe that these moral faculties are the grounds of responsibility, and the highest distinctions of human nature, and that no act is praiseworthy, any farther than it springs from their exertion. We believe, that no dispositions infused into us without our own moral activity, are of the nature of virtue, and therefore, we reject the doctrine of irresistible divine influence on the human mind, moulding it into good-

ness, as marble is hewn into a statue. Such goodness, if this word may be used, would not be the object of moral approbation, any more than the instinctive affections of inferior animals, or the constitutional amiableness of human beings.

By these remarks, we do not mean to deny the importance of God's aid or Spirit; but by his Spirit, we mean a moral, illuminating, and persuasive influence, not physical, not compulsory, not involving a necessity of virtue. We object, strongly, to the idea of many Christians respecting man's impotence and God's irresistible agency on the heart, believing that they subvert our responsibility and the laws of our moral nature, that they make men machines, that they cast on God the blame of all evil deeds, that they discourage good minds, and inflate the fanatical with wild conceits of immediate and sensible inspiration.

Among the virtues, we give the first place to the love of God. We believe, that this principle is the true end and happiness of our being, that we were made for union with our Creator, that his infinite perfection is the only sufficient object and true resting-place for the insatiable desires and unlimited capacities of the human mind, and that, without him, our noblest sentiments, admiration, veneration, hope, and love, would wither and decay. We believe, too, that the love of God is not only essential to happiness, but to the strength and perfection of all the virtues; that conscience, without the sanction of God's authority and retributive justice, would be a weak director; that benevolence, unless nourished by communion with his goodness, and encouraged by his smile, could not thrive amidst the selfishness and thanklessness of the world; and that self-government, without a sense of the divine inspection, would hardly extend beyond an outward and partial purity. God, as he is essentially goodness, holiness, justice, and virtue, so he is the life, motive, and sustainer of virtue in the human soul.

But, whilst we earnestly inculcate the love of God, we believe that great care is necessary to distinguish it from counterfeits. We think that much which is called piety is worthless. Many have fallen into the error, that there can be no excess in feelings which have God for their object; and, distrusting as coldness that self-possession, without which virtue and devotion lose all their dignity, they have abandoned themselves to extravagances, which have brought contempt on piety. Most certainly, if the love of God be that which often bears its name, the less we have of it the better. If religion be the shipwreck of understanding, we cannot keep too far from it. On this subject, we always speak plainly. We cannot sacrifice our reason to the reputation of zeal. We owe it to truth and religion to maintain, that fanaticism, partial insanity, sudden impressions, and ungovernable transports, are any thing rather than piety.

We conceive, that the true love of God is a moral sentiment, founded on a clear perception, and consisting in a high esteem and veneration, of his moral perfections. Thus, it perfectly coincides, and is in fact the same thing, with the love of virtue, rectitude, and goodness. You will easily judge, then, what we esteem the surest and only decisive signs of piety. We lay no stress on strong excitements. We esteem him, and him only a pious man, who practically conforms to God's moral perfections and government; who shows his delight in God's benevolence, by loving and serving his neighbour; his delight in God's justice, by being resolutely upright; his sense of God's purity, by regulating his thoughts, imagination, and desires; and whose conversation, business, and domestic life are swayed by a regard to

God's presence and authority. In all things else men may deceive themselves. Disordered nerves may give them strange sights, and sounds, and impressions. Texts of Scripture may come to them as from Heaven. Their whole souls may be moved, and their confidence in God's favor be undoubting. But in all this there is no religion. The question is, Do they love God's commands, in which his character is fully expressed, and give up to these their habits and passions? Without this, ecstasy is a mockery. One surrender of desire to God's will, is worth a thousand transports. We do not judge of the bent of men's minds by their raptures, any more than we judge of the natural direction of a tree during a storm. We rather suspect loud profession, for we have observed, that deep feeling is generally noiseless, and least seeks display.

We would not, by these remarks, be understood as wishing to exclude from religion warmth, and even transport. We honor, and highly value, true religious sensibility. We believe, that Christianity is intended to act powerfully on our whole nature, on the heart as well as the understanding and the conscience. We conceive of heaven as a state where the love of God will be exalted into an unbounded fervor and joy; and we desire, in our pilgrimage here, to drink into the spirit of that better world. But we think, that religious warmth is only to be valued, when it springs naturally from an improved character, when it comes unforced, when it is the recompense of obedience, when it is the warmth of a mind which understands God by being like him, and when, instead of disordering, it exalts the understanding, invigorates conscience, gives a pleasure to common duties, and is seen to exist in connexion with cheerfulness, judiciousness, and a reasonable frame of mind. When we observe a fervor, called religious, in men whose general character expresses little refinement and elevation, and whose piety seems at war with reason, we pay it little respect. We honor religion too much to give its sacred name to a feverish, forced, fluctuating zeal, which has little power over the life.

Another important branch of virtue, we believe to be love to Christ. The greatness of the work of Jesus, the spirit with which he executed it, and the sufferings which he bore for our salvation, we feel to be strong claims on our gratitude and veneration. We see in nature no beauty to be compared with the loveliness of his character, nor do we find on earth a benefactor to whom we owe an equal debt. We read his history with delight, and learn from it the perfection of our nature. We are particularly touched by his death, which was endured for our redemption, and by that strength of charity which triumphed over his pains. His resurrection is the foundation of our hope of immortality. His intercession gives us boldness to draw nigh to the throne of grace, and we look up to heaven with new desire, when we think, that, if we follow him here, we shall there see his benignant countenance, and enjoy his friendship for ever.

I need not express to you our views on the subject of the benevolent virtues. We attach such importance to these, that we are sometimes reproached with exalting them above piety. We regard the spirit of love, charity, meekness, forgiveness, liberality, and beneficence, as the badge and distinction of Christians, as the brightest image we can bear of God, as the best proof of piety. On this subject, I need not, and cannot enlarge; but there is one branch of benevolence which I ought not to pass over in silence, because we think that we conceive of it more highly and justly than many of

our brethren. I refer to the duty of candor, charitable judgment, especially towards those who differ in religious opinion. We think, that in nothing have Christians so widely
departed from their religion, as in this particular. We read
with astonishment and horror, the history of the church;
and sometimes when we look back on the fires of persecution, and on the zeal of Christians, in building up walls of
separation, and in giving up one another to perdition, we
feel as if we were reading the records of an infernal, rather
than a heavenly kingdom. An enemy to every religion, if
asked to describe a Christian, would, with some show of
reason, depict him as an idolater of his own distinguishing
opinions, covered with badges of party, shutting his eyes on
the virtues, and his ears on the arguments, of his opponents,
arrogating all excellence to his own sect and all saving power
to his own creed, sheltering under the name of pious zeal the
love of domination, the conceit of infallibility, and the spirit
of intolerance, and trampling on men's rights under the pretence of saving their souls.

We can hardly conceive of a plainer obligation on
beings of our frail and fallible nature, who are instructed in
the duty of candid judgment, than to abstain from condemning men of apparent conscientiousness and sincerity, who
are chargeable with no crime but that of differing from us
in the interpretation of the Scriptures, and differing, too, on
topics of great and acknowledged obscurity. We are astonished at the hardihood of those, who, with Christ's warnings
sounding in their ears, take on them the responsibility of
making creeds for his church, and cast out professors of
virtuous lives for imagined errors, for the guilt of thinking
for themselves. We know that zeal for truth is the cover for
this usurpation of Christ's prerogative; but we think that

zeal for truth, as it is called, is very suspicious, except in men, whose capacities and advantages, whose patient deliberation, and whose improvements in humility, mildness, and candor, give them a right to hope that their views are more just than those of their neighbours. Much of what passes for a zeal for truth, we look upon with little respect, for it often appears to thrive most luxuriantly where other virtues shoot up thinly and feebly; and we have no gratitude for those reformers, who would force upon us a doctrine which has not sweetened their own tempers, or made them better men than their neighbours.

We are accustomed to think much of the difficulties attending religious inquiries; difficulties springing from the slow development of our minds, from the power of early impressions, from the state of society, from human authority, from the general neglect of the reasoning powers, from the want of just principles of criticism and of important helps in interpreting Scripture, and from various other causes. We find, that on no subject have men, and even good men, ingrafted so many strange conceits, wild theories, and fictions of fancy, as on religion; and remembering, as we do, that we ourselves are sharers of the common frailty, we dare not assume infallibility in the treatment of our fellow-Christians, or encourage in common Christians, who have little time for investigation, the habit of denouncing and contemning other denominations, perhaps more enlightened and virtuous than their own. Charity, forbearance, a delight in the virtues of different sects, a backwardness to censure and condemn, these are virtues, which, however poorly practised by us, we admire and recommend; and we would rather join ourselves to the church in which they abound, than to any other communion, however elated with the belief of its own orthodoxy, however strict in guarding its creed, however burning with zeal against imagined error.

I have thus given the distinguishing views of those Christians in whose names I have spoken. We have embraced this system, not hastily or lightly, but after much deliberation; and we hold it fast, not merely because we believe it to be true, but because we regard it as purifying truth, as a doctrine according to godliness, as able to "work mightily" and to "bring forth fruit" in them who believe. That we wish to spread it, we have no desire to conceal; but we think, that we wish its diffusion, because we regard it as more friendly to practical piety and pure morals than the opposite doctrines, because it gives clearer and nobler views of duty, and stronger motives to its performance, because it recommends religion at once to the understanding and the heart, because it asserts the lovely and venerable attributes of God, because it tends to restore the benevolent spirit of Jesus to his divided and afflicted church, and because it cuts off every hope of God's favor, except that which springs from practical conformity to the life and precepts of Christ. We see nothing in our views to give offence, save their purity, and it is their purity, which makes us seek and hope their extension through the world.

My friend and brother;—You are this day to take upon you important duties; to be clothed with an office, which the Son of God did not disdain; to devote yourself to that religion, which the most hallowed lips have preached, and the most precious blood sealed. We trust that you will bring to this work a willing mind, a firm purpose, a martyr's spirit, a readiness to toil and suffer for the truth, a devotion of your best powers to the interests of piety and virtue. I have spoken of the doctrines which you will probably preach; but I do not mean, that you are to give yourself to controversy. You will remember, that good practice is the end of preaching, and will labor to make your people holy livers, rather than skilful disputants. Be careful, lest the desire of defending what you deem truth, and of repelling reproach and misrepresentation, turn you aside from your great business, which is to fix in men's minds a living conviction of the obligation, sublimity, and happiness of Christian virtue. The best way to vindicate your sentiments, is to show, in your preaching and life, their intimate connexion with Christian morals, with a high and delicate sense of duty, with candor towards your opposers, with inflexible integrity, and with an habitual reverence for God. If any light can pierce and scatter the clouds of prejudice, it is that of a pure example. My brother, may your life preach more loudly than your lips. Be to this people a pattern of all good works, and may your instructions derive authority from a well-grounded belief in your hearers, that you speak from the heart, that you preach from experience, that the truth which you dispense has wrought powerfully in your own heart, that God, and Jesus, and heaven, are not merely words on your lips, but most affecting realities to your mind, and springs of hope and consolation, and strength, in all your trials. Thus laboring, may you reap abundantly, and have a testimony of your faithfulness, not only in your own conscience, but in the esteem, love, virtues, and improvements of your people.

To all who hear me, I would say, with the Apostle, Prove all things, hold fast that which is good. Do not, brethren, shrink from the duty of searching God's Word for yourselves, through fear of human censure and denunciation. Do not think, that you may innocently follow the opinions which prevail around you, without investigation, on the ground, that Christianity is now so purified from errors, as to need no laborious research. There is much reason to believe, that Christianity is at this moment dishonored by gross and cherished corruptions. If you remember the darkness which hung over the Gospel for ages; if you consider the impure union, which still subsists in almost every Christian country, between the church and state, and which enlists men's selfishness and ambition on the side of established error; if you recollect in what degree the spirit of intolerance has checked free inquiry, not only before, but since the Reformation; you will see that Christianity cannot have freed itself from all the human inventions, which disfigured it under the Papal tyranny. No. Much stubble is yet to be burned; much rubbish to be removed; many gaudy decorations, which a false taste has hung around Christianity, must be swept away; and the earth-born fogs, which have long shrouded it, must be scattered, before this divine fabric will rise before us in its native and awful majesty, in its harmonious proportions, in its mild and celestial splendors. This glorious reformation in the church, we hope, under God's blessing, from the progress of the human intellect, from the moral progress of society, from the consequent decline of prejudice and bigotry, and, though last not least, from the subversion of human authority in matters of religion, from the fall of those hierarchies, and other human institutions, by which the minds of individuals are oppressed under the weight of numbers, and a Papal dominion is perpetuated in the Protestant church. Our earnest prayer to God is, that he will overturn, and overturn, and overturn the strong-holds of spiritual usurpation, until HE shall come, whose right it is to rule the minds of men; that the conspiracy of ages against the liberty of Christians may be brought to an end; that the servile assent, so long yielded to human creeds, may give place to honest and devout inquiry into the Scriptures; and that Christianity, thus purified from error, may put forth its almighty energy, and prove itself, by its ennobling influence on the mind, to be indeed "the power of God unto salvation."

THE DIVINITY SCHOOL ADDRESS

By Ralph Waldo Emerson

Delivered before the Senior Class at the Harvard Divinity School, Cambridge on July 15, 1838.

In this refulgent summer, it has been a luxury to draw the breath of life. The grass grows, the buds burst, the meadow is spotted with fire and gold in the tint of flowers. The air is full of birds, and sweet with the breath of the pine, the balm-of-Gilead, and the new hay. Night brings no gloom to the heart with its welcome shade. Through the transparent darkness the stars pour their almost spiritual rays. Man under them seems a young child, and his huge globe a toy. The cool night bathes the world as with a river, and prepares his eyes again for the crimson dawn. The mystery of nature was never displayed more happily. The corn and the wine have been freely dealt to all creatures, and the never-broken silence with which the old bounty goes forward, has not yielded yet one word of explanation. One is constrained to respect the perfection of this world, in which our senses converse. How wide; how rich; what invitation from every property it gives to every faculty of man! In its fruitful soils; in its navigable sea; in its mountains of metal and stone; in its forests of all woods; in its animals; in its chemical ingredients; in the powers and path of light, heat, attraction, and life, it is well worth the pith and heart of great men to subdue and enjoy it. The planters, the mechanics, the inventors, the astronomers, the builders of cities, and the captains, history delights to honor.

But when the mind opens, and reveals the laws which traverse the universe, and make things what they are, then shrinks the great world at once into a mere illustration and fable of this mind. What am I? and What is? asks the human spirit with a curiosity new-kindled, but never to be quenched. Behold these out-running laws, which our imperfect apprehension can see tend this way and that, but not come full circle. Behold these infinite relations, so like, so unlike; many, yet one. I would study, I would know, I would admire forever. These works of thought have been the entertainments of the human spirit in all ages.

A more secret, sweet, and overpowering beauty appears to man when his heart and mind open to the sentiment of virtue. Then he is instructed in what is above him. He learns that his being is without bound; that, to the good, to the perfect, he is born, low as he now lies in evil and weakness. That which he venerates is still his own, though he has not realized it yet. *He ought.* He knows the sense of that grand word, though his analysis fails entirely to render account of it. When in innocency, or when by intellectual perception, he attains to say,—'I love the Right; Truth is beautiful within and without, forevermore. Virtue, I am thine: save me: use me: thee will I serve, day and night, in great, in small, that I may be not virtuous, but virtue;'— then is the end of the creation answered, and God is well pleased.

The sentiment of virtue is a reverence and delight in

the presence of certain divine laws. It perceives that this
homely game of life we play, covers, under what seem fool-
ish details, principles that astonish. The child amidst his
baubles, is learning the action of light, motion, gravity, mus-
cular force; and in the game of human life, love, fear, justice,
appetite, man, and God, interact. These laws refuse to be
adequately stated. They will not be written out on paper, or
spoken by the tongue. They elude our persevering thought;
yet we read them hourly in each other's faces, in each other's
actions, in our own remorse. The moral traits which are all
globed into every virtuous act and thought,—in speech, we
must sever, and describe or suggest by painful enumeration
of many particulars. Yet, as this sentiment is the essence of
all religion, let me guide your eye to the precise objects of
the sentiment, by an enumeration of some of those classes of
facts in which this element is conspicuous.

The intuition of the moral sentiment is an insight of the
perfection of the laws of the soul. These laws execute themselves. They are out of time, out of space, and not subject
to circumstance. Thus; in the soul of man there is a justice
whose retributions are instant and entire. He who does a
good deed, is instantly ennobled. He who does a mean deed,
is by the action itself contracted. He who puts off impurity,
thereby puts on purity. If a man is at heart just, then in so
far is he God; the safety of God, the immortality of God, the
majesty of God do enter into that man with justice. If a
man dissemble, deceive, he deceives himself, and goes out of
acquaintance with his own being. A man in the view of
absolute goodness, adores, with total humility. Every step
so downward, is a step upward. The man who renounces
himself, comes to himself.

See how this rapid intrinsic energy worketh everywhere,

righting wrongs, correcting appearances, and bringing up facts to a harmony with thoughts. Its operation in life, though slow to the senses, is, at last, as sure as in the soul. By it, a man is made the Providence to himself, dispensing good to his goodness, and evil to his sin. Character is always known. Thefts never enrich; alms never impoverish; murder will speak out of stone walls. The least admixture of a lie,—for example, the taint of vanity, the least attempt to make a good impression, a favorable appearance,—will instantly vitiate the effect. But speak the truth, and all nature and all spirits help you with unexpected furtherance. Speak the truth, and all things alive or brute are vouchers, and the very roots of the grass underground there, do seem to stir and move to bear you witness. See again the perfection of the Law as it applies itself to the affections, and becomes the law of society. As we are, so we associate. The good, by affinity, seek the good; the vile, by affinity, the vile. Thus of their own volition, souls proceed into heaven, into hell.

These facts have always suggested to man the sublime creed, that the world is not the product of manifold power, but of one will, of one mind; and that one mind is everywhere active, in each ray of the star, in each wavelet of the pool; and whatever opposes that will, is everywhere balked and baffled, because things are made so, and not otherwise. Good is positive. Evil is merely privative, not absolute: it is like cold, which is the privation of heat. All evil is so much death or nonentity. Benevolence is absolute and real. So much benevolence as a man hath, so much life hath he. For all things proceed out of this same spirit, which is differently named love, justice, temperance, in its different applications, just as the ocean receives different names on the several shores which it washes. All things proceed out of the same spirit, and all things conspire with it. Whilst a man seeks good ends, he is strong by the whole strength of nature. In so far as he roves from these ends, he bereaves himself of power, of auxiliaries; his being shrinks out of all remote channels, he becomes less and less, a mote, a point, until absolute badness is absolute death.

The perception of this law of laws awakens in the mind a sentiment which we call the religious sentiment, and which makes our highest happiness. Wonderful is its power to charm and to command. It is a mountain air. It is the embalmer of the world. It is myrrh and storax, and chlorine and rosemary. It makes the sky and the hills sublime, and the silent song of the stars is it. By it, is the universe made safe and habitable, not by science or power. Thought may work cold and intransitive in things, and find no end or unity; but the dawn of the sentiment of virtue on the heart, gives and is the assurance that Law is sovereign over all natures; and the worlds, time, space, eternity, do seem to break out into joy.

This sentiment is divine and deifying. It is the beatitude of man. It makes him illimitable. Through it, the soul first knows itself. It corrects the capital mistake of the infant man, who seeks to be great by following the great, and hopes to derive advantages *from another*,—by showing the fountain of all good to be in himself, and that he, equally with every man, is an inlet into the deeps of Reason. When he says, "I ought;" when love warms him; when he chooses, warned from on high, the good and great deed; then, deep melodies wander through his soul from Supreme Wisdom. Then he can worship, and be enlarged by his worship; for he can never go behind this sentiment. In the sublimest flights of the soul, rectitude is never surmounted, love is never outgrown.

This sentiment lies at the foundation of society, and successively creates all forms of worship. The principle of veneration never dies out. Man fallen into superstition, into sensuality, is never quite without the visions of the moral sentiment. In like manner, all the expressions of this sentiment are sacred and permanent in proportion to their purity. The expressions of this sentiment affect us more than all other compositions. The sentences of the oldest time, which ejaculate this piety, are still fresh and fragrant. This thought dwelled always deepest in the minds of men in the devout and contemplative East; not alone in Palestine, where it reached its purest expression, but in Egypt, in Persia, in India, in China. Europe has always owed to oriental genius, its divine impulses. What these holy bards said, all sane men found agreeable and true. And the unique impression of Jesus upon mankind, whose name is not so much written as ploughed into the history of this world, is proof of the subtle virtue of this infusion.

Meantime, whilst the doors of the temple stand open, night and day, before every man, and the oracles of this truth cease never, it is guarded by one stern condition; this, namely; it is an intuition. It cannot be received at second hand. Truly speaking, it is not instruction, but provocation, that I can receive from another soul. What he announces, I must find true in me, or wholly reject; and on his word, or as his second, be he who he may, I can accept nothing. On the contrary, the absence of this primary faith is the presence of degradation. As is the flood so is the ebb. Let this faith depart, and the very words it spake, and the things it made, become false and hurtful. Then falls the church, the state,

art, letters, life. The doctrine of the divine nature being forgotten, a sickness infects and dwarfs the constitution. Once
man was all; now he is an appendage, a nuisance. And
because the indwelling Supreme Spirit cannot wholly be got
rid of, the doctrine of it suffers this perversion, that the
divine nature is attributed to one or two persons, and denied
to all the rest, and denied with fury. The doctrine of inspiration is lost; the base doctrine of the majority of voices,
usurps the place of the doctrine of the soul. Miracles, prophecy, poetry; the ideal life, the holy life, exist as ancient
history merely; they are not in the belief, nor in the aspira-
tion of society; but, when suggested, seem ridiculous. Life
is comic or pitiful, as soon as the high ends of being fade
out of sight, and man becomes near-sighted, and can only
attend to what addresses the senses.

These general views, which, whilst they are general,
none will contest, find abundant illustration in the history
of religion, and especially in the history of the Christian
church. In that, all of us have had our birth and nurture.
The truth contained in that, you, my young friends, are now
setting forth to teach. As the Cultus, or established worship
of the civilized world, it has great historical interest for us.
Of its blessed words, which have been the consolation of
humanity, you need not that I should speak. I shall en-
deavor to discharge my duty to you, on this occasion, by
pointing out two errors in its administration, which daily
appear more gross from the point of view we have just now
taken.

Jesus Christ belonged o the true race of prophets. He
saw with open eye the mystery of the soul. Drawn by its
severe harmony, ravished with its beauty, he lived in it, and
had his being there. Alone in all history, he estimated the

uniqueness of JC nt in = "Son of God" but that he saw
all of us as children of God w equal opportunity for
access.

Ralph Waldo Emerson   97

greatness of man. One man was true to what is in you and
me. He saw that God incarnates himself in man, and evermore goes forth anew to take possession of his world. He
said, in this jubilee of sublime emotion, 'I am divine.
Through me, God acts; through me, speaks. Would you see
God, see me; or, see thee, when thou also thinkest as I now
think.' But what a distortion did his doctrine and memory
suffer in the same, in the next, and the following ages! There
is no doctrine of the Reason which will bear to be taught by
the Understanding. The understanding caught this high
chant from the poet's lips, and said, in the next age, 'This
was Jehovah come down out of heaven. I will kill you, if
you say he was a man.' The idioms of his language, and the
figures of his rhetoric, have usurped the place of his truth;
and churches are not built on his principles, but on his
tropes. Christianity became a Mythus, as the poetic teaching of Greece and of Egypt, before. He spoke of miracles;
for he felt that man's life was a miracle, and all that man
doth, and he knew that this daily miracle shines, as the
character ascends. But the word Miracle, as pronounced by
Christian churches, gives a false impression; it is Monster.
It is not one with the blowing clover and the falling rain.

He felt respect for Moses and the prophets; but no
unfit tenderness at postponing their initial revelations, to
the hour and the man that now is; to the eternal revelation
in the heart. Thus was he a true man. Having seen that the
law in us is commanding, he would not suffer it to be commanded. Boldly, with hand, and heart, and life, he declared
it was God. Thus is he, as I think, the only soul in history
who has appreciated the worth of a man.

1. In this point of view we become very sensible of the
first defect of historical Christianity. Historical Christianity

has fallen into the error that corrupts all attempts to communicate religion. As it appears to us, and as it has appeared for ages, it is not the doctrine of the soul, but an exaggeration of the personal, the positive, the ritual. It has dwelt, it dwells, with noxious exaggeration about the *person* of Jesus. The soul knows no persons. It invites every man to expand to the full circle of the universe, and will have no preferences but those of spontaneous love. But by this eastern monarchy of a Christianity, which indolence and fear have built, the friend of man is made the injurer of man. The manner in which his name is surrounded with expressions, which were once sallies of admiration and love, but are now petrified into official titles, kills all generous sympathy and liking. All who hear me, feel, that the language that describes Christ to Europe and America, is not the style of friendship and enthusiasm to a good and noble heart, but is appropriated and formal,—paints a demigod, as the Orientals or the Greeks would describe Osiris or Apollo. Accept the injurious impositions of our early catechetical instruction, and even honesty and self-denial were but splendid sins, if they did not wear the Christian name. One would rather be

'A pagan, suckled in a creed outworn,'

than to be defrauded of his manly right in coming into nature, and finding not names and places, not land and professions, but even virtue and truth foreclosed and monopolized. You shall not be a man even. You shall not own the world; you shall not dare, and live after the infinite Law that is in you, and in company with the infinite Beauty which heaven and earth reflect to you in all lovely forms; but you must subordinate your nature to Christ's nature; you must accept our interpretations; and take his portrait as the vulgar draw it.

That is always best which gives me to myself. The sublime is excited in me by the great stoical doctrine, Obey thyself. That which shows God in me, fortifies me. That which shows God out of me, makes me a wart and a wen. There is no longer a necessary reason for my being. Already the long shadows of untimely oblivion creep over me, and I shall decease forever.

The divine bards are the friends of my virtue, of my intellect, of my strength. They admonish me, that the gleams which flash across my mind, are not mine, but God's; that they had the like, and were not disobedient to the heavenly vision. So I love them. Noble provocations go out from them, inviting me to resist evil; to subdue the world; and to Be. And thus by his holy thoughts, Jesus serves us, and thus only. To aim to convert a man by miracles, is a profanation of the soul. A true conversion, a true Christ, is now, as always, to be made, by the reception of beautiful sentiments. It is true that a great and rich soul, like his, falling among the simple, does so preponderate, that, as his did, it names the world. The world seems to them to exist for him, and they have not yet drunk so deeply of his sense, as to see that only by coming again to themselves, or to God in themselves, can they grow forevermore. It is a low benefit to give me something; it is a high benefit to enable me to do somewhat of myself. The time is coming when all men will see, that the gift of God to the soul is not a vaunting, over-powering, excluding sanctity, but a sweet, natural goodness, a goodness like thine and mine, and that so invites thine and mine to be and to grow.

The injustice of the vulgar tone of preaching is not less

flagrant to Jesus, than to the souls which it profanes. The preachers do not see that they make his gospel not glad, and shear him of the locks of beauty and the attributes of heaven. When I see a majestic Epaminondas, or Washington; when I see among my contemporaries, a true orator, an upright judge, a dear friend; when I vibrate to the melody and fancy of a poem; I see beauty that is to be desired. And so lovely, and with yet more entire consent of my human being, sounds in my ear the severe music of the bards that have sung of the true God in all ages. Now do not degrade the life and dialogues of Christ out of the circle of this charm, by insulation and peculiarity. Let them lie as they befel, alive and warm, part of human life, and of the landscape, and of the cheerful day.

2. The second defect of the traditionary and limited way of using the mind of Christ is a consequence of the first; this, namely; that the Moral Nature, that Law of laws, whose revelations introduce greatness,—yea, God himself, into the open soul, is not explored as the fountain of the established teaching in society. Men have come to speak of the revelation as somewhat long ago given and done, as if God were dead. The injury to faith throttles the preacher; and the goodliest of institutions becomes an uncertain and inarticulate voice.

It is very certain that it is the effect of conversation with the beauty of the soul, to beget a desire and need to impart to others the same knowledge and love. If utterance is denied, the thought lies like a burden on the man. Always the seer is a sayer. Somehow his dream is told: somehow he publishes it with solemn joy: sometimes with pencil on canvas; sometimes with chisel on stone; sometimes in towers and aisles of granite, his soul's worship is builded; sometimes in anthems of indefinite music; but clearest and most permanent, in words.

The man enamored of this excellency, becomes its priest or poet. The office is coeval with the world. But observe the condition, the spiritual limitation of the office. The spirit only can teach. Not any profane man, not any sensual, not any liar, not any slave can teach, but only he can give, who has; he only can create, who is. The man on whom the soul descends, through whom the soul speaks, alone can teach. Courage, piety, love, wisdom, can teach; and every man can open his door to these angels, and they shall bring him the gift of tongues. But the man who aims to speak as books enable, as synods use, as the fashion guides, and as interest commands, babbles. Let him hush.

To this holy office, you propose to devote yourselves. I wish you may feel your call in throbs of desire and hope. The office is the first in the world. It is of that reality, that it cannot suffer the deduction of any falsehood. And it is my duty to say to you, that the need was never greater of new revelation than now. From the views I have already expressed, you will infer the sad conviction, which I share, I believe, with numbers, of the universal decay and now almost death of faith in society. The soul is not preached. The Church seems to totter to its fall, almost all life extinct. On this occasion, any complaisance would be criminal, which told you, whose hope and commission it is to preach the faith of Christ, that the faith of Christ is preached.

It is time that this ill-suppressed murmur of all thoughtful men against the famine of our churches; this moaning of the heart because it is bereaved of the consolation, the hope, the grandeur, that come alone out of the culture of the moral nature; should be heard through the sleep of indolence, and

over the din of routine. This great and perpetual office of
the preacher is not discharged. Preaching is the expression
of the moral sentiment in application to the duties of life.
In how many churches, by how many prophets, tell me, is
man made sensible that he is an infinite Soul; that the earth
and heavens are passing into his mind; that he is drinking
forever the soul of God? Where now sounds the persuasion,
that by its very melody imparadises my heart, and so affirms
its own origin in heaven? Where shall I hear words such as
in elder ages drew men to leave all and follow,—father and
mother, house and land, wife and child? Where shall I hear
these august laws of moral being so pronounced, as to fill my
ear, and I feel ennobled by the offer of my uttermost action
and passion? The test of the true faith, certainly, should be
its power to charm and command the soul, as the laws of nature control the activity of the hands,—so commanding that
we find pleasure and honor in obeying. The faith should
blend with the light of rising and of setting suns, with the
flying cloud, the singing bird, and the breath of flowers. But
now the priest's Sabbath has lost the splendor of nature; it
is unlovely; we are glad when it is done; we can make, we
do make, even sitting in our pews, a far better, holier,
sweeter, for ourselves.

Whenever the pupit is usurped by a formalist, then is
the worshipper defrauded and disconsolate. We shrink as
soon as the prayers begin, which do not uplift, but smite and
offend us. We are fain to wrap our cloaks about us, and
secure, as best we can, a solitude that hears not. I once
heard a preacher who sorely tempted me to say, I would go
to church no more. Men go, thought I, where they are wont
to go, else had no soul entered the temple in the afternoon.
A snow storm was falling around us. The snow storm was

real; the preacher merely spectral; and the eye felt the sad contrast in looking at him, and then out of the window behind him, into the beautiful meteor of the snow. He had lived in vain. He had no one word intimating that he had laughed or wept, was married or in love, had been commended, or cheated, or chagrined. If he had ever lived and acted, we were none the wiser for it. The capital secret of his profession, namely, to convert life into truth, he had not learned. Not one fact in all his experience, had he yet imported into his doctrine. This man had ploughed, and planted, and talked, and bought, and sold; he had read books; he had eaten and drunken; his head aches; his heart throbs; he smiles and suffers; yet was there not a surmise, a hint, in all the discourse, that he had ever lived at all. Not a line did he draw out of real history. The true preacher can be known by this, that he deals out to the people his life,— life passed through the fire of thought. But of the bad preacher, it could not be told from his sermon, what age of the world he fell in; whether he had a father or a child; whether he was a freeholder or a pauper; whether he was a citizen or a countryman; or any other fact of his biography. It seemed strange that the people should come to church. It seemed as if their houses were very unentertaining, that they should prefer this thoughtless clamor. It shows that there is a commanding attraction in the moral sentiment, that can lend a faint tint of light to dulness and ignorance, coming in its name and place. The good hearer is sure he has been touched sometimes; is sure there is somewhat to be reached, and some word that can reach it. When he listens to these vain words, he comforts himself by their relation to his remembrance of better hours, and so they clatter and echo unchallenged.

I am not ignorant that when we preach unworthily, it is not always quite in vain. There is a good ear, in some men, that draws supplies to virtue out of very indifferent nutriment. There is poetic truth concealed in all the common-places of prayer and of sermons, and though foolishly spoken, they may be wisely heard; for, each is some select expression that broke out in a moment of piety from some stricken or jubilant soul, and its excellency made it remembered. The prayers and even the dogmas of our church, are like the zodiac of Denderah, and the astronomical monuments of the Hindoos, wholly insulated from anything now extant in the life and business of the people. They mark the height to which the waters once rose. But this docility is a check upon the mischief from the good and devout. In a large portion of the community, the religious service gives rise to quite other thoughts and emotions. We need not chide the negligent servant. We are struck with pity, rather, at the swift retribution of his sloth. Alas for the unhappy man that is called to stand in the pulpit, and *not* give bread of life. Everything that befalls, accuses him. Would he ask contributions for the missions, foreign or domestic? Instantly his face is suffused with shame, to propose to his parish, that they should send money a hundred or a thousand miles, to furnish such poor fare as they have at home, and would do well to go the hundred or the thousand miles to escape. Would he urge people to a godly way of living;— and can he ask a fellow-creature to come to Sabbath meetings, when he and they all know what is the poor uttermost they can hope for therein? Will he invite them privately to the Lord's Supper? He dares not. If no heart warm this rite, the hollow, dry, creaking formality is too plain, than that he can face a man of wit and energy, and put the invitation

without terror. In the street, what has he to say to the bold
village blasphemer? The village blasphemer sees fear in the
face, form, and gait of the minister.

Let me not taint the sincerity of this plea by any over-
sight of the claims of good men. I know and honor the
purity and strict conscience of numbers of the clergy. What
life the public worship retains, it owes to the scattered company of pious men, who minister here and there in the
churches, and who, sometimes accepting with too great
tenderness the tenet of the elders, have not accepted from
others, but from their own heart, the genuine impulses of
virtue, and so still command our love and awe, to the sanctity of character. Moreover, the exceptions are not so much
to be found in a few eminent preachers, as in the better
hours, the truer inspirations of all,—nay, in the sincere
moments of every man. But with whatever exception, it is
still true, that tradition characterizes the preaching of this
country; that it comes out of the memory, and not out of
the soul; that it aims at what is usual, and not at what is
necessary and eternal; that thus, historical Christianity destroys the power of preaching, by withdrawing it from the
exploration of the moral nature of man, where the sublime
is, where are the resources of astonishment and power.
What a cruel injustice it is to that Law, the joy of the whole
earth, which alone can make thought dear and rich; that
Law whose fatal sureness the astronomical orbits poorly
emulate, that it is travestied and depreciated, that it is be-
hooted and behowled, and not a trait, not a word of it
articulated. The pulpit in losing sight of this Law, loses its
reason, and gropes after it knows not what. And for want
of this culture, the soul of the community is sick and faith-
less. It wants nothing so much as a stern, high, stoical,

Christian discipline, to make it know itself and the divinity
that speaks through it. Now man is ashamed of himself; he
skulks and sneaks through the world, to be tolerated, to be
pitied, and scarcely in a thousand years does any man dare
to be wise and good, and so draw after him the tears and
blessings of his kind.

Certainly there have been periods when, from the in-
activity of the intellect on certain truths, a greater faith was
possible in names and persons. The Puritans in England and
America, found in the Christ of the Catholic Church, and
in the dogmas inherited from Rome, scope for their austere
piety, and their longings for civil freedom. But their creed
is passing away, and none arises in its room. I think no
man can go with his thoughts about him, into one of our
churches, without feeling, that what hold the public worship
had on men is gone, or going. It has lost its grasp on the
affection of the good, and the fear of the bad. In the
country, neighborhoods, half parishes are *signing off*,—to
use the local term. It is already beginning to indicate character and religion to withdraw from the religious meetings.
I have heard a devout person, who prized the Sabbath, say
in bitterness of heart, "On Sundays, it seems wicked to go to
church." And the motive, that holds the best there, is now
only a hope and a waiting. What was once a mere circumstance, that the best and the worst men in the parish, the
poor and the rich, the learned and the ignorant, young and
old, should meet one day as fellows in one house, in sign of
an equal right in the soul,—has come to be a paramount
motive for going thither.

My friends, in these two errors, I think, I find the
causes of a decaying church and a wasting unbelief. And
what greater calamity can fall upon a nation, than the loss

of worship? Then all things go to decay. Genius leaves the temple, to haunt the senate, or the market. Literature becomes frivolous. Science is cold. The eye of youth is not lighted by the hope of other worlds, and age is without honor. Society lives to trifles, and when men die, we do not mention them.

And now, my brothers, you will ask, What in these desponding days can be done by us? The remedy is already declared in the ground of our complaint of the Church. We have contrasted the Church with the Soul. In the soul, then, let the redemption be sought. Wherever a man comes, there comes revolution. The old is for slaves. When a man comes, all books are legible, all things transparent, all religions are forms. He is religious. Man is the wonderworker. He is seen amid miracles. All men bless and curse. He saith yea and nay, only. The stationariness of religion; the assumption that the age of inspiration is past, that the Bible is closed; the fear of degrading the character of Jesus by representing him as a man; indicate with sufficient clearness the falsehood of our theology. It is the office of a true teacher to show us that God is, not was; that He speaketh, not spake. The true Christianity,—a faith like Christ's in the infinitude of man,—is lost. None believeth in the soul of man, but only in some man or person old and departed. Ah me! no man goeth alone. All men go in flocks to this saint or that poet, avoiding the God who seeth in secret. They cannot see in secret; they love to be blind in public. They think society wiser than their soul, and know not that one soul, and their soul, is wiser than the whole world. See how nations and races flit by on the sea of time, and leave no ripple to tell where they floated or sunk, and one good soul shall make the name of Moses, or of Zeno, or of Zoroaster, reverend forever. None assayeth the stern ambition to be the Self of the nation, and of nature, but each would be an easy secondary to some Christian scheme, or sectarian connection, or some eminent man. Once leave your own knowledge of God, your own sentiment, and take secondary knowledge, as St. Paul's, or George Fox's, or Swedenborg's, and you get wide from God with every year this secondary form lasts, and if, as now, for centuries,—the chasm yawns to that breadth, that men can scarcely be convinced there is in them anything divine.

Let me admonish you, first of all, to go alone; to refuse the good models, even those which are sacred in the imagination of men, and dare to love God without mediator or veil. Friends enough you shall find who will hold up to your emulation Wesleys and Oberlins, Saints and Prophets. Thank God for these good men, but say, 'I also am a man.' Imitation cannot go above its model. The imitator dooms himself to hopeless mediocrity. The inventor did it, because it was natural to him, and so in him it has a charm. In the imitator, something else is natural, and he bereaves himself of his own beauty, to come short of another man's.

Yourself a newborn bard of the Holy Ghost,—cast behind you all conformity, and acquaint men at first hand with Deity. Look to it first and only, that fashion, custom, authority, pleasure, and money, are nothing to you,—are not bandages over your eyes, that you cannot see,—but live with the privilege of the immeasurable mind. Not too anxious to visit periodically all families and each family in your parish connection,—when you meet one of these men or women, be to them a divine man; be to them thought and virtue; let their timid aspirations find in you a friend; let their trampled instincts be genially tempted out in your atmosphere; let their doubts know that you have doubted, and their wonder feel that you have wondered. By trusting your own heart, you shall gain more confidence in other men. For all our penny-wisdom, for all our soul-destroying slavery to habit, it is not to be doubted, that all men have sublime thoughts; that all men value the few real hours of life; they love to be heard; they love to be caught up into the vision of principles. We mark with light in the memory the few interviews we have had, in the dreary years of routine and of sin, with souls that made our souls wiser; that spoke what we thought; that told us what we knew; that gave us leave to be what we inly were. Discharge to men the priestly office, and, present or absent, you shall be followed with their love as by an angel.

And, to this end, let us not aim at common degrees of merit. Can we not leave, to such as love it, the virtue that glitters for the commendation of society, and ourselves pierce the deep solitudes of absolute ability and worth? We easily come up to the standard of goodness in society. Society's praise can be cheaply secured, and almost all men are content with those easy merits; but the instant effect of conversing with God, will be, to put them away. There are persons who are not actors, not speakers, but influences; persons too great for fame, for display; who disdain eloquence; to whom all we call art and artist, seems too nearly allied to show and by-ends, to the exaggeration of the finite and selfish, and loss of the universal. The orators, the poets, the commanders encroach on us only as fair women do, by our allowance and homage. Slight them by preoccupation of mind, slight them, as you can well afford to do, by high and universal aims, and they instantly feel that you have right, and that it is in lower places that they must shine. They

also feel your right; for they with you are open to the influx
of the all-knowing Spirit, which annihilates before its broad
noon the little shades and gradations of intelligence in the
compositions we call wiser and wisest.

In such high communion, let us study the grand strokes
of rectitude: a bold benevolence, an independence of friends,
so that not the unjust wishes of those who love us, shall im-
pair our freedom, but we shall resist for truth's sake the
freest flow of kindness, and appeal to sympathies far in
advance; and,—what is the highest form in which we know
this beautiful element,—a certain solidity of merit, that has
nothing to do with opinion, and which is so essentially and
manifestly virtue, that it is taken for granted, that the right,
the brave, the generous step will be taken by it, and nobody
thinks of commending it. You would compliment a cox-
comb doing a good act, but you would not praise an angel.
The silence that accepts merit as the most natural thing in
the world, is the highest applause. Such souls, when they
appear, are the Imperial Guard of Virtue, the perpetual reserve, the dictators of fortune. One needs not praise their
courage,—they are the heart and soul of nature. O my
friends, there are resources in us on which we have not
drawn. There are men who rise refreshed on hearing a
threat; men to whom a crisis which intimidates and paralyzes
the majority,—demanding not the faculties of prudence and
thrift, but comprehension, immovableness, the readiness of
sacrifice,—comes graceful and beloved as a bride. Napoleon
said of Massena, that he was not himself until the battle
began to go against him; then, when the dead began to fall
in ranks around him, awoke his powers of combination, and
he put on terror and victory as a robe. So it is in rugged

crises, in unweariable endurance, and in aims which put sympathy out of question, that the angel is shown. But these are heights that we can scarce remember and look up to, without contrition and shame. Let us thank God that such things exist.

And now let us do what we can to rekindle the smouldering, nigh quenched fire on the altar. The evils of the church that now is are manifest. The question returns, What shall we do? I confess, all attempts to project and establish a Cultus with new rites and forms, seem to me vain. Faith makes us, and not we it, and faith makes its own forms. All attempts to contrive a system are as cold as the new worship introduced by the French to the goddess of Reason,—to-day, pasteboard and fillagree, and ending tomorrow in madness and murder. Rather let the breath of new life be breathed by you through the forms already existing. For, if once you are alive, you shall find they shall become plastic and new. The remedy to their deformity is, first, soul, and second, soul, and evermore, soul. A whole popedom of forms, one pulsation of virtue can uplift and vivify. Two inestimable advantages Christianity has given us; first; the Sabbath, the jubilee of the whole world; whose light dawns welcome alike into the closet of the philosopher, into the garret of toil, and into prison cells, and everywhere suggests, even to the vile, the dignity of spiritual being. Let it stand forevermore, a temple, which new love, new faith, new sight shall restore to more than its first splendor to mankind. And secondly, the institution of preaching,—the speech of man to men,—essentially the most flexible of all organs, of all forms. What hinders that now, everywhere, in pulpits, in lecture-rooms, in houses, in fields, wherever the invitation of men or your own occasions lead you, you speak the very truth, as your life and conscience teach it, and cheer the waiting, fainting hearts of men with new hope and new revelation?

I look for the hour when that supreme Beauty, which ravished the souls of those eastern men, and chiefly of those Hebrews, and through their lips spoke oracles to all time, shall speak in the West also. The Hebrew and Greek Scriptures contain immortal sentences, that have been bread of life to millions. But they have no epical integrity; are fragmentary; are not shown in their order to the intellect. I look for the new Teacher, that shall follow so far those shining laws, that he shall see them come full circle; shall see their rounding complete grace; shall see the world to be the mirror of the soul; shall see the identity of the law of gravitation with purity of heart; and shall show that the Ought, that Duty, is one thing with Science, with Beauty, and with Joy.

THE TRANSIENT AND PERMANENT IN CHRISTIANITY

By Theodore Parker

Delivered at the Ordination of Rev. Charles C. Shackford in the Hawes Place Church, Boston on May 19, 1841.

LUKE XXI. 33. "Heaven and earth shall pass away: but my word shall not pass away."

In this sentence we have a very clear indication that Jesus of Nazareth believed the religion he taught would be eternal, that the substance of it would last forever. Yet there are some, who are affrighted by the faintest rustle which a heretic makes among the dry leaves of theology; they tremble lest Christianity itself should perish without hope. Ever and anon the cry is raised, "The Philistines be upon us. and Christianity is in danger." The least doubt respecting the popular theology, or the existing machinery of the church; the least sign of distrust in the Religion of the Pulpit, or the Religion of the Street, is by some good men supposed to be at enmity with faith in Christ, and capable of shaking Christianity itself. On the other hand, a few bad men and a few pious men, it is said, on both sides of the water, tell us the day of Christianity is past. The latter—it is alleged—would persuade us that, hereafter, Piety must take a new form; the teachings of Jesus are to be passed by; that Religion is to wing her way sublime, above the flight of Christianity, far away, toward heaven, as the fledged eaglet leaves forever the nest which sheltered his callow youth. Let us, therefore, devote a few moments to this subject, and consider what is *Transient* in Christianity, and what is *Permanent* therein. The topic seems not inappropriate to the times in which we live, or the occasion that calls us together.

Christ says, his Word shall never pass away. Yet at first sight nothing seems more fleeting than a word. It is an evanescent impulse of the most fickle element. It leaves no track where it went through the air. Yet to this, and this only, did Jesus entrust the truth wherewith he came laden, to the earth; truth for the salvation of the world. He took no pains to perpetuate his thoughts; they were poured forth where occasion found him an audience,—by the side of the lake, or a well; in a cottage, or the temple; in a fisher's boat, or the synagogue of the Jews. He founds no institution as a monument of his words. He appoints no order of men to preserve his bright and glad revelations. He only bids his friends give freely the truth they had freely received. He did not even write his words in a book. With a noble confidence, the result of his abiding faith, he scattered them broad-cast on the world, leaving the seed to its own vitality. He knew, that what is of God cannot fail, for God keeps his own. He sowed his seed in the heart, and left it there, to be watered and warmed by the dew and the sun which heaven sends. He felt his words were for eternity. So he trusted them to

the uncertain air; and for eighteen hundred years that faithful element has held them good,—distinct as when first
warm from his lips. Now they are translated into every human speech, and mumured in all earth's thousand tongues,
from the pine forests of the North to the palm groves of eastern Ind. They mingle, as it were, with the roar of a populous
city, and join the chime of the desert sea. Of a Sabbath
morn they are repeated from church to church, from isle to
isle, and land to land, till their music goes round the world.
These words have become the breath of the good, the hope
of the wise, the joy of the pious, and that for many millions
of hearts. They are the prayers of our churches; our better
devotion by fireside and fieldside; the enchantment of our
hearts. It is these words, that still work wonders, to which
the first recorded miracles were nothing in grandeur and
utility. It is these, which build our temples and beautify our
homes. They raise our thoughts of sublimity; they purify
our ideal of purity: they hallow our prayer for truth and
love. They make beauteous and divine the life which plain
men lead. They give wings to our aspirations. What charm-
ers they are! Sorrow is lulled at their bidding. They take
the sting out of disease, and rob adversity of his power to
disappoint. They give health and wings to the pious soul,
broken-hearted and shipwrecked in his voyage through life,
and encourage him to tempt the perilous way once more.
They make all things ours: Christ our brother; Time our
servant; Death our ally and the witness of our triumph.
They reveal to us the presence of God, which else we might
not have seen so clearly, in the first wind-flower of spring;
in the falling of a sparrow; in the distress of a nation; in the
sorrow or the rapture of the world. Silence the voice of
Christianity, and the world is well nigh dumb, for gone is

that sweet music which kept in awe the rulers and the people, which cheers the poor widow in her lonely toil, and comes like light through the windows of morning, to men who sit stooping and feeble, with failing eyes and a hungering heart. It is gone—all gone! only the cold, bleak world left before them.

Such is the life of these Words; such the empire they have won for themselves over men's minds since they were spoken first. In the mean time, the words of great men and mighty, whose name shook whole continents, though graven in metal and stone, though stamped in institutions and defended by whole tribes of priests and troops of followers— their words have gone to the ground, and the world gives back no echo of their voice. Meanwhile the great works also of old times. castle and tower and town, their cities and their empires, have perished, and left scarce a mark on the bosom of the earth to show they once have been. The philosophy of the wise, the art of the accomplished, the song of the poet, the ritual of the priest, though honored as divine in their day, have gone down, a prey to oblivion. Silence has closed over them; only their spectres now haunt the earth. A deluge of blood has swept over the nations; a night of darkness, more deep than the fabled darkness of Egypt, has lowered down upon that flood, to destroy or to hide what the deluge had spared. But through all this, the words of Christianity have come down to us from the lips of that Hebrew youth, gentle and beautiful as the light of a star, not spent by their journey through time and through space. They have built up a new civilization, which the wisest Gentile never hoped for; which the most pious Hebrew never foretold. Through centuries of wasting, these words have flown on, like a dove in the storm, and now wait to descend on hearts pure and earnest,

as the Father's spirit, we are told, came down on his lowly
Son. The old heavens and the old earth are indeed passed
away, but the Word stands. Nothing shows clearer than this,
how fleeting is what man calls great; how lasting what God
pronounces true.

Looking at the Word of Jesus, at real Christianity, the
pure religion he taught, nothing appears more fixed and certain. Its influence widens as light extends; it deepens as
the nations grow more wise. But, looking at the history of
what men call Christianity, nothing seems more uncertain
and perishable. While true religion is always the same
thing, in each century and every land, in each man that feels
it, the Christianity of the Pulpit, which is the religion taught;
the Christianity of the People, which is the religion that is
accepted and lived out; has never been the same thing in
any two centuries or lands, except only in name. The
difference between what is called Christianity by the Unitarians in our times, and that of some ages past, is greater
than the difference between Mahomet and the Messiah. The
difference at this day between opposing classes of Christians;
the difference between the Christianity of some sects, and
that of Christ himself; is deeper and more vital than that
between Jesus and Plato, Pagan as we call him. The
Christianity of the seventh century has passed away. We
recognise only the ghost of Superstition in its faded features,
as it comes up at our call. It is one of the things which has
been, and can be no more, for neither God nor the world
goes back. Its terrors do not frighten, nor its hopes allure
us. We rejoice that it has gone. But how do we know that
our Christianity shall not share the same fate? Is there that
difference between the nineteenth century, and some seven-

teen that have gone before it, since Jesus, to warrant the belief that our notion of Christianity shall last forever? The stream of time has already beat down Philosophies and Theologies, Temple and Church, though never so old and revered. How do we know there is not a perishing element in what we call Christianity? Jesus tells us, *his* Word is the word of God, and so shall never pass away. But who tells us, that *our* word shall never pass away? that *our notion* of his Word shall stand forever?

Let us look at this matter a little more closely. In actual Christianity—that is, in that portion of Christianity which is preached and believed—there seem to have been, ever since the time of its earthly founder, two elements, the one transient, the other permanent. The one is the thought, the folly, the uncertain wisdom, the theological notions, the impiety of man; the other, the eternal truth of God. These two bear perhaps the same relation to each other that the phenomena of outward nature, such as sunshine and cloud, growth, decay, and reproduction, bear to the great law of nature, which underlies and supports them all. As in that case, more attention is commonly paid to the particular phenomena than to the general law; so in this case, more is generally given to the Transient in Christianity than to the Permanent therein.

It must be confessed, though with sorrow, that transient things form a great part of what is commonly taught as Religion. An undue place has often been assigned to forms and doctrines, while too little stress has been laid on the divine life of the soul, love to God, and love to man. Religious forms may be useful and beautiful. They are so, whenever they speak to the soul, and answer a want thereof.

In our present state some forms are perhaps necessary. But they are only the accident of Christianity; not its substance. They are the robe, not the angel, who may take another robe, quite as becoming and useful. One sect has many forms; another none. Yet both may be equally Christian, in spite of the redundance or the deficiency. They are a part of the language in which religion speaks, and exist, with few exceptions, wherever man is found. In our calculating nation, in our rationalizing sect, we have retained but two of the rites so numerous in the early Christian church, and even these we have attenuated to the last degree, leaving them little more than a spectre of the ancient form. Another age may continue or forsake both; may revive old forms, or invent new ones to suit the altered circumstances of the times, and yet be Christians quite as good as we, or our fathers of the dark ages. Whether the Apostles designed these rites to be perpetual, seems a question which belongs to scholars and antiquarians; not to us, as Christian men and women. So long as they satisfy or help the pious heart, so long they are good. Looking behind, or around us, we see that the forms and rites of the Christians are quite as fluctuating as those of the heathens; from whom some of them have been, not unwisely, adopted by the earlier church.

Again, the doctrines that have been connected with Christianity, and taught in its name, are quite as changeable as the form. This also takes place unavoidably. If observations be made upon Nature,—which must take place so long as man has senses and understanding,—there will be a philosophy of Nature, and philosophical doctrines. These will differ as the observations are just or inaccurate, and as the deductions from observed facts are true or false. Hence there will be different schools of natural philosophy, so long as men have eyes and understandings of different clearness and strength. And if men observe and reflect upon Religion,—which will be done so long as man is a religious and reflective being,—there must also be a philosophy of religion, a theology and theological doctrines. These will differ, as men have felt much or little of religion, as they analyze their sentiments correctly or otherwise, and as they have reasoned right or wrong. Now the true system of Nature which exists in the outward facts, whether discovered or not, is always the same thing, though the philosophy of Nature, which men invent, change every month, and be one thing at London and the opposite at Berlin. Thus there is but one system of Nature as it exists in fact, though many theories of Nature, which exist in our imperfect notions of that system, and by which we may approximate and at length reach it. Now there can be but one Religion which is absolutely true, existing in the facts of human nature, and the ideas of Infinite God. That, whether acknowledged or not, is always the same thing and never changes. So far as a man has any real religion—either the principle or the sentiment thereof—so far he has that, by whatever name he may call it. For, strictly speaking, there is but one kind of religion, as there is but one kind of love, though the manifestations of this religion, in forms, doctrines, and life, be never so diverse. It is through these, men approximate to the true expression of this religion. Now while this religion is one and always the same thing, there may be numerous systems of theology or philosophies of religion. These with their creeds, confessions, and collections of doctrines, deduced by reasoning upon the facts observed, may be baseless and false, either because the observation was too narrow in extent, or otherwise defective in point of accuracy, or because the reasoning was illogical, and therefore the deduction spurious. Each of these three faults is conspicuous in the systems of theology. Now the solar system as it exists in fact is permanent, though the notions of Thales and Ptolemy, of Copernicus and Descartes about this system, prove transient, imperfect approximations to the true expression. So the Christianity of Jesus is permanent, though what passes for Christianity with Popes and catechisms, with sects and churches, in the first century or in the nineteenth century, prove transient also. Now it has sometimes happened that a man took his philosophy of Nature at second hand, and then attempted to make his observations conform to his theory, and Nature ride in his panniers. Thus some philosophers refused to look at the Moon through Galileo's telescope, for, according to their theory of vision, such an instrument would not aid the sight. Thus their preconceived notions stood up between them and Nature. Now it has often happened that men took their theology thus at second hand, and distorted the history of the world and man's nature besides, to make Religion conform to their notions. Their theology stood between them and God. Those obstinate philosophers have disciples in no small number.

What another has said of false systems of science, will apply equally to the popular theology: "It is barren in effects, fruitful in questions, slow and languid in its improvement, exhibiting in its generality the counterfeit of perfection, but ill filled up in its details, popular in its choice, but suspected by its very promoters, and therefore bolstered up and countenanced with artifices. Even those who have been determined to try for themselves, to add their support to learning, and to enlarge its limits, have not dared entirely to desert received opinions, nor to seek the spring-head of things. But they think they have done a great thing if they intersperse and contribute something of their own; prudently considering, that by their assent they can save their modesty, and by their contributions, their liberty. Neither is there, nor ever will be, an end or limit to these things. One snatches at one thing, another is pleased with another; there is no dry nor clear sight of anything. Every one plays the philosopher out of the small treasures of his own fancy. The more sublime wits more acutely and with better success; the duller with less success but equal obstinacy, and, by the discipline of some learned men, sciences are bounded within the limits of some certain authors which they have set down, imposing them upon old men and instilling them into young. So that now (as Tully cavilled upon Cæsar's consulship) the star Lyra riseth by an edict, and authority is taken for truth and not truth for authority; which kind of order and discipline is very convenient for our present use, but banisheth those which are better."

Any one, who traces the history of what is called Christianity, will see that nothing changes more from age to age than the doctrines taught as Christian, and insisted on as essential to Christianity and personal salvation. What is falsehood in one province passes for truth in another. The heresy of one age is the orthodox belief and "only infallible rule" of the next. Now Arius, and now Athanasius is Lord of the ascendant. Both were excommunicated in their turn, each for affirming what the other denied. Men are burned for professing what men are burned for denying. For centuries the doctrines of the Christians were no better, to say the least, than those of their contemporary pagans. The theological doctrines derived from our fathers seem to have come from Judaism, Heathenism, and the caprice of philosophers, far more than they have come from the principle and sentiment of Christianity. The doctrine of the Trinity, the very Achilles of theological dogmas, belongs to philosophy and not religion; its subtleties cannot even be expressed in our tongue. As old religions became superannuated and died out, they left to the rising faith, as to a residuary legatee, their forms and their doctrines; or rather, as the giant in the fable left his poisoned garment to work the overthrow of his conqueror. Many tenets, that pass current in our theology, seem to be the refuse of idol temples; the offscourings of Jewish and heathen cities, rather than the sands of virgin gold, which the stream of Christianity has worn off from the rock of ages, and brought in its bosom for us. It is wood, hay, and stubble, wherewith men have built on the corner stone Christ laid. What wonder the fabric is in peril when tried by fire? The stream of Christianity, as men receive it, has caught a stain from every soil it has filtered through, so that now it is not the pure water from the well of Life, which is offered to our lips, but streams troubled and polluted by man with mire and dirt. If Paul and Jesus could read our books of theological doctrines, would they accept as their teaching, what men have vented in their name? Never till the letters of Paul had faded out of his memory; never till the words of Jesus had been torn out from the Book of Life. It is their notions about Christianity men have taught as the only living word of God. They have piled their own rubbish against the temple of Truth where Piety comes up to worship; what wonder the pile seems unshapely and like to fall? But these theological doctrines are fleeting as the leaves on the trees. They

"Are found
Now green in youth, now withered on the ground;
Another race the following spring supplies;
They fall successive and successive rise."

Like the clouds of the sky, they are here to-day; to-morrow, all swept off and vanished; while Christianity itself, like the heaven above, with its sun, and moon, and uncounted stars, is always over our head, though the cloud sometimes debars us of the needed light. It must of necessity be the case that our reasonings, and therefore our theological doctrines, are imperfect, and so perishing. It is only gradually that we approach to the true system of Nature by observation and reasoning, and work out our philosophy and theology by the toil of the brain. But meantime, if we are faithful, the great truths of morality and religion, the deep sentiment of love to man and love to God, are perceived intuitively, and by instinct, as it were, though our theology be imperfect and miserable. The theological notions of Abraham, to take the story as it stands, were exceedingly gross, yet a greater than Abraham has told us Abraham desired to see my day, saw it, and was glad. Since these notions are so fleeting, why need we accept the commandment of men, as the doctrine of God?

This transitoriness of doctrines appears, in many instances, of which two may be selected for a more attentive consideration. First, the doctrine respecting the origin and authority of the Old and New Testament. There has been a time when men were burned for asserting doctrines of natural philosophy, which rested on evidence the most incontestable, because those doctrines conflicted with sentences in the Old Testament. Every word of that Jewish

record was regarded as miraculously inspired, and therefore
as infallibly true. It was believed that the Christian religion
itself rested thereon, and must stand or fall with the immaculate Hebrew text. He was deemed no small sinner who
found mistakes in the manuscripts. On the authority of the
written Word, man was taught to believe impossible legends,
conflicting assertions; to take fiction for fact; a dream for
a miraculous revelation of God; an oriental poem for a grave
history of miraculous events; a collection of amatory idyls
for a serious discourse "touching the mutual love of Christ
and the Church;" they have been taught to accept a picture
sketched by some glowing eastern imagination, never intended to be taken for a reality, as a proof that the Infinite
God spoke in human words, appeared in the shape of a
cloud, a flaming bush, or a man who ate, and drank, and
vanished into smoke; that he gave counsels to-day, and the
opposite to-morrow; that he violated his own laws; was
angry, and was only dissuaded by a mortal man from de-
stroying at once a whole nation—millions of men who re-
belled against their leader in a moment of anguish. Questions in philosophy, questions in the Christian religion, have
been settled by an appeal to that book. The inspiration of
its authors has been assumed as infallible. Every fact in the
early Jewish history has been taken as a type of some anal-
ogous fact in Christian history. The most distant events,
even such as are still in the arms of time, were supposed
to be clearly foreseen and foretold by pious Hebrews several
centuries before Christ. It has been assumed at the outset,
with no shadow of evidence, that those writers held a
miraculous communication with God, such as he has granted
to no other man. What was originally a presumption of
bigoted Jews became an article of faith, which Christians

were burned for not believing. This has been for centuries the general opinion of the Christian church, both Catholic and Protestant, though the former never accepted the Bible as the *only* source of religious truth. It has been so. Still worse, it is now the general opinion of religious sects at this day. Hence the attempt, which always fails, to reconcile the philosophy of our times with the poems in Genesis writ a thousand years before Christ; hence the attempt to conceal the contradictions in the record itself. Matters have come to such a pass, that even now he is is deemed an infidel, if not by implication an atheist, whose reverence for the Most High forbids him to believe that God commanded Abraham to sacrifice his Son, a thought at which the flesh creeps with horror; to believe it solely on the authority of an oriental story, written down nobody knows when or by whom, or for what purpose; which may be a poem, but cannot be the record of a fact, unless God is the author of confusion and a lie.

Now this idolatry of the Old Testament has not always existed. Jesus says that none born of a woman is greater than John the Baptist, yet the least in the kingdom of heaven was greater than John. Paul tells us the Law—the very crown of the old Hebrew revelation—is a shadow of good things, which have now come; only a schoolmaster to bring us to Christ, and when faith has come, that we are no longer under the schoolmaster; that it was a law of sin and death, from which we are made free by the Law of the spirit of Life. Christian teachers themselves have differed so widely in their notion of the doctrines and meaning of those books, that it makes one weep to think of the follies deduced therefrom. But modern Criticism is fast breaking to pieces this idol which men have made out of the Scriptures. It

has shown that here are the most different works thrown together. That their authors, wise as they sometimes were;
pious as we feel often their spirit to have been, had only
that inspiration which is common to other men equally pious
and wise; that they were by no means infallible; but were
mistaken in facts or in reasoning; uttered predictions which
time has not fulfilled; men who in some measure partook of
the darkness and limited notions of their age, and were not
always above its mistakes or its corruptions.

The history of opinions on the New Testament is quite
similar. It has been assumed at the outset, it would seem
with no sufficient reason, without the smallest pretence on
its writers' part, that all of its authors were infallibly and
miraculously inspired, so that they could commit no error of
doctrine or fact. Men have been bid to close their eyes at
the obvious difference between Luke and John; the serious
disagreement between Paul and Peter; to believe, on the
smallest evidence, accounts which shock the moral sense and
revolt the reason, and tend to place Jesus in the same series
with Hercules, and Apollonius of Tyana; accounts which
Paul in the Epistles never mentions, though he also had a
vein of the miraculous running quite through him. Men
have been told that all these things must be taken as part of
Christianity, and if they accepted the religion, they must
take all these accessories along with it; that the living spirit
could not be had without the killing letter. All the books,
which caprice or accident had brought together between the
lids of the Bible, were declared to be the infallible word of
God; the only certain rule of religious faith and practice.
Thus the Bible was made not a single channel, but the *only*
certain rule of religious faith and practice. To disbelieve
any of its statements, or even the common interpretation

put upon those statements by the particular age or church in which the man belonged, was held to be infidelity if not atheism. In the name of him who forbid us to judge our brother, good men and pious men have applied these terms to others, good and pious as themselves. That state of things has by no means passed away. Men, who cry down the absurdities of Paganism in the worst spirit of the French "free-thinkers," call others infidels and atheists, who point out, though reverently, other absurdities which men have piled upon Christianity. So the world goes. An idolatrous regard for the imperfect scripture of God's word, is the apple of Atalanta, which defeats theologians running for the hand of divine truth.

But the current notions respecting the infallible inspiration of the Bible have no foundation in the Bible itself. Which Evangelist, which Apostle of the New Testament, what Prophet or Psalmist of the Old Testament, ever claims infallible authority for himself or for others? Which of them does not in his own writings show that he was finite, and with all his zeal and piety, possessed but a limited inspiration, the bound whereof we can sometimes discover? Did Christ ever demand that men should assent to the doctrines of the Old Testament, credit its stories, and take its poems for histories, and believe equally two accounts that contradict one another? Has he ever told you that all the truths of his religion, all the beauty of a Christian life should be contained in the writings of those men, who, even after his resurrection, expected him to be a Jewish king; of men who were sometimes at variance with one another and misunderstood his divine teachings? Would not those modest writers themselves be confounded at the idolatry we pay them? Opinions may change on these points, as they have often changed—changed greatly and for the worse since the days of Paul. They are changing now, and we may hope for the better; for God makes man's folly as well as his wrath to praise Him, and continually brings good out of evil.

Another instance of the transitoriness of doctrines, taught as Christian, is found in those which relate to the nature and authority of Christ. One ancient party has told us, that he is the infinite God; another, that he is both God and man; a third, that he was a man, the son of Joseph and Mary,—born as we are; tempted like ourselves; inspired, as we may be, if we will pay the price. Each of the former parties believed its doctrine on this head was infallibly true, and formed the very substance of Christianity, and was one of the essential conditions of salvation, though scarce any two distinguished teachers, of ancient or modern times, agree in their expression of this truth.

Almost every sect, that has ever been, makes Christianity rest on the personal authority of Jesus, and not the immutable truth of the doctrines themselves, or the authority of God, who sent him into the world. Yet it seems difficult to conceive any reason, why moral and religious truths should rest for their support on the personal authority of their revealer, any more than the truths of science on that of him who makes them known first or most clearly. It is hard to see why the great truths of Christianity rest on the personal authority of Jesus, more than the axioms of geometry rest on the personal authority of Euclid, or Archimedes. The authority of Jesus, as of all teachers, one would naturally think, must rest on the truth of his words, and not their truth on his authority.

Opinions respecting the nature of Christ seem to be

constantly changing. In the three first centuries after Christ, it appears, great latitude of speculation prevailed. Some said he was God, with nothing of human nature, his body only an illusion; others, that he was man, with nothing of the divine nature, his miraculous birth having no foundation in fact. In a few centuries it was decreed by councils that he was God, thus honoring the divine element; next, that he was man also, thus admitting the human side. For some ages the Catholic Church seems to have dwelt chiefly on the divine nature that was in him, leaving the human element to mystics and other heretical persons, whose bodies served to flesh the swords of orthodox believers. The stream of Christianity has come to us in two channels—one within the Church, the other without the Church—and it is not hazarding too much to say, that since the fourth century the true Christian life has been out of the established Church, and not in it, but rather in the ranks of dissenters. From the Reformation till the latter part of the last century, we are told, the Protestant Church dwelt chiefly on the human side of Christ, and since that time many works have been written to show how the two—perfect Deity and perfect manhood —were united in his character. But, all this time, scarce any two eminent teachers agree on these points, however orthodox they may be called. What a difference between the Christ of John Gerson and John Calvin,—yet were both accepted teachers and pious men. What a difference between the Christ of the Unitarians and the Methodists— yet may men of both sects be true Christians and acceptable with God. What a difference between the Christ of Matthew and John—yet both were disciples, and their influence is wide as Christendom and deep as the heart of man. But on this there is not time to enlarge.

Now it seems clear, that the notion men form about the origin and nature of the scriptures; respecting the nature and authority of Christ, have nothing to do with Christianity except as its aids or its adversaries; they are not the foundation of its truths. These are theological questions; not religious questions. Their connection with Christianity appears accidental; for if Jesus had taught at Athens, and not at Jerusalem; if he had wrought no miracle, and none but the human nature had ever been ascribed to him; if the Old Testament had forever perished at his birth,—Christianity would still have been the Word of God; it would have lost none of its truths. It would be just as true, just as beautiful, just as lasting, as now it is; though we should have lost so many a blessed word, and the work of Christianity itself would have been, perhaps, a long time retarded.

To judge the future by the past, the former authority of the Old Testament can never return. Its present authority cannot stand. It must be taken for what it is worth. The occasional folly and impiety of its authors must pass for no more than their value;—while the religion, the wisdom, the love, which make fragrant its leaves, will still speak to the best hearts as hitherto, and in accents even more divine, when Reason is allowed her rights. The ancient belief in the infallible inspiration of each sentence of the New Testament is fast changing; very fast. One writer, not a skeptic, but a Christian of unquestioned piety, sweeps off the beginning of Matthew; another, of a different church and equally religious, the end of John. Numerous critics strike off several epistles. The Apocalypse itself it not spared, notwithstanding its concluding curse. Who shall tell us the work of retrenchment is to stop here; that others will not demonstrate, what some pious hearts have long felt, that errors of doctrine and errors of fact may be found in many parts of the record, here and there, from the beginning of Matthew to the end of Acts? We see how opinions have changed ever since the apostles' time; and who shall assure us that they were not sometimes mistaken in historical, as well as doctrinal matters; did not sometimes confound the actual with the imaginary; and that the fancy of these pious writers never stood in the place of their recollection?

But what if this should take place? Is Christianity then to perish out of the heart of the nations, and vanish from the memory of the world, like the religions that were before Abraham? It must be so, if it rest on a foundation which a scoffer may shake, and a score of pious critics shake down. But this is the foundation of a theology, not of Christianity. That does not rest on the decision of Councils. It is not to stand or fall with the infallible inspiration of a few Jewish fishermen, who have writ their names in characters of light all over the world. It does not continue to stand through the forbearance of some critic, who can cut, when he will, the thread on which its life depends. Christianity does not rest on the infallible authority of the New Testament. It depends on this collection of books for the historical statement of its facts. In this we do not require infallible inspiration on the part of the writers, more than in the record of other historical facts. To me it seems as presumptuous, on the one hand, for the believer to claim this evidence for the truth of Christianity, as it is absurd, on the other hand, for the skeptic to demand such evidence to support these historical statements. I cannot see that it depends on the personal authority of Jesus. He was the organ through which the Infinite spoke. It is God that was manifested in the flesh by him, on whom rests the truth which Jesus brought to light and made clear and beautiful in his life; and if Christianity be true, it seems useless to look for any other authority to uphold it, as for some one to support Almighty God. So if it could be proved,—as it cannot,—in opposition to the greatest amount of historical evidence ever collected on any similar point, that the gospels were the fabrication of designing and artful men, that Jesus of Nazareth had never lived, still Christianity would stand firm, and fear no evil. None of the doctrines of that religion would fall to the ground; for if true, they stand by themselves. But we should lose,—oh, irreparable loss!—the example of that character, so beautiful, so divine, that no human genius could have conceived it, as none, after all the progress and refinement of eighteen centuries, seems fully to have comprehended its lustrous life. If Christianity were true, we should still think it was so, not because its record was written by infallible pens; nor because it was lived out by an infallible teacher,—but that it is true, like the axioms of geometry, because it is true, and is to be tried by the oracle God places in the breast. If it rest on the personal authority of Jesus alone, then there is no certainty of its truth, if he were ever mistaken in the smallest matter, as some Christians have thought he was, in predicting his second coming.

These doctrines respecting the scriptures have often changed, and are but fleeting. Yet men lay much stress on them. Some cling to these notions as if they were Christianity itself. It is about these and similar points that theological battles are fought from age to age. Men sometimes use worst the choicest treasure which God bestows. This is especially true of the use men make of the Bible. Some men have regarded it as the heathen their idol, or the savage his fetish. They have subordinated Reason, Conscience, and Religion to this. Thus have they lost half the treasure it bears in its bosom. No doubt the time will come when its true character shall be felt. Then it will be seen, that, amid all the contradictions of the Old Testament; its legends so beautiful as fictions, so appalling as facts; amid its predictions that have never been fulfilled; amid the puerile conceptions of God, which sometimes occur, and the cruel denunciations that disfigure both Psalm and Prophecy, there is a reverence for man's nature, a sublime trust in God, and a depth of piety rarely felt in these cold northern hearts of ours. Then the devotion of its authors, the loftiness of their aim, and the majesty of their life, will appear doubly fair, and Prophet and Psalmist will warm our hearts as never before. Their voice will cheer the young and sanctify the gray-headed; will charm us in the toil of life, and sweeten the cup Death gives us, when he comes to shake off this mantle of flesh. Then will it be seen, that the words of Jesus are the music of heaven, sung in an earthly voice, and the echo of these words in John and Paul owe their efficacy to their truth and their depth, and to no accidental matter connected therewith. Then can the Word,—which was in the beginning and now is,—find access to the innermost heart of man, and speak there as now it seldom speaks. Then shall the Bible,—which is a whole library of the deepest and most earnest thoughts and feelings and piety and love, ever recorded in human speech,—be read oftener than ever before, not with Superstition, but with Reason, Conscience, and Faith fully active. Then shall it sustain men bowed down with many sorrows; rebuke sin; encourage virtue; sow the world broad-cast and quick with the seed of love, that man may reap a harvest for life everlasting.

With all the obstacles men have thrown in its path, how much has the Bible done for mankind. No abuse has deprived us of all its blessings. You trace its path across the world from the day of Pentecost to this day. As a river springs up in the heart of a sandy continent, having its father in the skies and its birth-place in distant, unknown mountains; as the stream rolls on, enlarging itself, making in that arid waste a belt of verdure, wherever it turns its way; creating palm groves and fertile plains, where the smoke of the cottager curls up at even-tide, and marble cities send the gleam of their splendor far into the sky;—such has been the course of the Bible on the earth. Despite of idolaters bowing to the dust before it, it has made a deeper mark on the world than the rich and beautiful literature of all the heathen. The first book of the Old Testament tells man he is made in the image of God; the first of the New Testament gives us the motto, Be perfect as your Father in heaven. Higher words were never spoken. How the truths of the Bible have blest us. There is not a boy on all the hills of New England; not a girl born in the filthiest cellar which disgraces a capital in Europe, and cries to God against the barbarism of modern civilization; not a boy nor a girl all Christendom through, but their lot is made better by that great book.

Doubtless the time will come when men shall see Christ also as he is. Well might he still say: "Have I been so long with you, and yet hast thou not known me?" No! we have made him an idol, have bowed the knee before him, saying, "Hail, king of the Jews;" called him "Lord, Lord!" but done not the things which he said. The history of the Christian world might well be summed up in one word of the evangelist—"and there they crucified him," for there has never been an age when men did not crucify the Son of God afresh. But if error prevail for a time and grow old in the world, truth will triumph at the last, and then we shall see the Son of God as he is. Lifted up he shall draw all nations unto him. Then will men understand the Word of Jesus, which shall not pass away. Then shall we see and love the divine life that he lived. How vast has his influence been. How his spirit wrought in the hearts of his disciples, rude, selfish, bigoted, as at first they were. How it has wrought in the world. His words judge the nations. The wisest son of man has not measured their height. They speak to what is deepest in profound men; what is holiest in good men; what is divinest in religious men. They kindle anew the flame of devotion in hearts long cold. They are Spirit and Life. His truth was not derived from Moses and Solomon; but the light of God shone through him, not colored, not bent aside. His life is the perpetual rebuke of all time since. It condemns ancient civilization; it condemns modern civilization. Wise men we have since had, and good men; but this Galilean youth strode before the world whole thousands of years,—so much of Divinity was in him. His words solve the questions of this present age. In him the Godlike and the Human met and embraced, and a divine Life was born. Measure him by the world's greatest sons; —how poor they are. Try him by the best of men,—how little and low they appear. Exalt him as much as we may, we shall yet, perhaps, come short of the mark. But still was he not our brother; the son of man, as we are; the Son of God, like ourselves? His excellence, was it not human excellence? His wisdom, love, piety,—sweet and celestial as they were, —are they not what we also may attain? In him, as in a

mirror, we may see the image of God, and go on from glory
to glory, till we are changed into the same image, led by the
spirit which enlightens the humble. Viewed in this way, how
beautiful is the life of Jesus. Heaven has come down to
earth, or rather, earth has become heaven. The Son of
God, come of age, has taken possession of his birthright.
The brightest revelation is this,—of what is possible for all
men, if not now at least hereafter. How pure is his spirit,
and how encouraging its words. "Lowly sufferer," he
seems to say, "see how I bore the cross. Patient laborer,
be strong; see how I toiled for the unthankful and the merci-
less. Mistaken sinner, see of what thou art capable. Rise
up, and be blessed."

But if, as some early Christians began to do, you take a
heathen view, and make him a God, the Son of God in a
peculiar and exclusive sense—much of the significance of
his character is gone. His virtue has no merit; his love no
feeling; his cross no burthen; his agony no pain. His death
is an illusion; his resurrection but a show. For if he were
not a man, but a god, what are all these things; what his
words, his life, his excellence of achievement?—It is all
nothing, weighed against the illimitable greatness of Him
who created the worlds and fills up all time and space!
Then his resignation is no lesson; his life no model; his
death no triumph to you or me,—who are not gods, but
mortal men, that know not what a day shall bring forth, and
walk by faith "dim sounding on our perilous way." Alas,
we have despaired of man, and so cut off his brightest hope.

In respect of doctrines as well as forms we see all is
transitory. "Every where is instability and insecurity."
Opinions have changed most, on points deemed most vital.

Could we bring up a Christian teacher of any age,—from the sixth to the fourteenth century, for example, though a teacher of undoubted soundness of faith, whose word filled the churches of Christendom, clergymen would scarce allow him to kneel at their altar, or sit down with them at the Lord's table. His notions of Christianity could not be expressed in our forms; nor could our notions be made intelligible to his ears. The questions of his age, those on which Christianity was thought to depend,—questions which perplexed and divided the subtle doctors,—are no questions to us. The quarrels which then drove wise men mad, now only excite a smile or a tear, as we are disposed to laugh or weep at the frailty of man. We have other straws of our own to quarrel for. Their ancient books of devotion do not speak to us; their theology is a vain word. To look back but a short period, the theological speculations of our fathers during the last two centuries; their "practical divinity;" even the sermons written by genius and piety, are, with rare exceptions, found unreadable; such a change is there in the doctrines.

Now who shall tell us that the change is to stop here? That this sect or that, or even all sects united, have exhausted the river of life, and received it all in their canonized urns, so that we need draw no more out of the eternal well, but get refreshment nearer at hand? Who shall tell us that another age will not smile at our doctrines, disputes, and unchristian quarrels about Christianity, and make wide the mouth at men who walked brave in orthodox raiment, delighting to blacken the names of heretics, and repeat again the old charge "he hath blasphemed"? Who shall tell us they will not weep at the folly of all such as fancied Truth shone only into the contracted nook of their school, or sect, or coterie? Men of other times may look down equally on the heresy-hunters, and men hunted for heresy, and wonder at both. The men of all ages before us, were quite as confident as we, that their opinion was truth; that their notion was Christianity and the whole thereof. The men who lit the fires of persecution, from the first martyr to Christian bigotry down to the last murder of the innocents, had no doubt their opinion was divine. The contest about transubstantiation, and the immaculate purity of the Hebrew and Greek texts of the scriptures, was waged with a bitterness unequalled in these days. The Protestant smiles at one, the Catholic at the other, and men of sense wonder at both. It might teach us all a lesson, at least of forbearance. No doubt, an age will come, in which ours shall be reckoned a period of darkness—like the sixth century—when men groped for the wall but stumbled and fell, because they trusted a transient notion, not an eternal truth; an age when temples were full of idols, set up by human folly, an age in which Christian light had scarce begun to shine into men's hearts. But while this change goes on; while one generation of opinions passes away, and another rises up; Christianity itself, that pure Religion, which exists eternal in the constitution of the soul and the mind of God, is always the same. The Word that was before Abraham, in the very beginning, will not change, for that word is Truth. From this Jesus subtracted nothing; to this he added nothing. But he came to reveal it as the secret of God, that cunning men could not understand, but which filled the souls of men meek and lowly of heart. This truth we owe to God; the revelation thereof to Jesus, our elder brother, God's chosen son.

To turn away from the disputes of the Catholics and the Protestants, of the Unitarian and the Trinitarian, of Old School and New School, and come to the plain words of Jesus of Nazareth, Christianity is a simple thing; very simple. It is absolute, pure Morality; absolute, pure Religion; the love of man; the love of God acting without let or hindrance. The only creed it lays down is the great truth which springs up spontaneous in the holy heart—there is a God. Its watchword is, be perfect as your Father in Heaven. The only form it demands is a divine life; doing the best thing, in the best way, from the highest motives; perfect obedience to the great law of God. Its sanction is the voice of God in your heart; the perpetual presence of Him, who made us and the stars over our head; Christ and the Father abiding within us. All this is very simple; a little child can understand it; very beautiful, the loftiest mind can find nothing so lovely. Try it by Reason, Conscience, and Faith—things highest in man's nature—we see no redundance, we feel no deficiency. Examine the particular duties it enjoins; humility, reverence, sobriety, gentleness, charity, forgiveness, fortitude, resignation, faith, and active love; try the whole extent of Christianity so well summed up in the command, "Thou shalt love the Lord thy God with all thy heart, and with all thy soul, and with all thy mind—thou shalt love thy neighbor as thyself;" and is there anything therein that can perish? No, the very opponents of Christianity have rarely found fault with the teachings of Jesus. The end of Christianity seems to be to make all men one with God as Christ was one with Him; to bring them to such a state of obedience and goodness, that we shall think divine thoughts and feel divine sentiments, and so keep the law of God by living a life of truth and love. Its means are Purity and Prayer; getting strength from God and using it for our fellow men as well as ourselves. It allows perfect freedom. It does not demand all men to *think* alike, but to think uprightly, and get as near as possible at truth; not all men to *live* alike, but to live holy, and get as near as possible to a life perfectly divine. Christ set up no pillars of Hercules, beyond which men must not sail the sea in quest of truth. He says, "I have many things to say unto you, but ye cannot bear them now . . . Greater works than these shall ye do." Christianity lays no rude hand on the sacred peculiarity of individual genius and character. But there is no Christian sect which does not fetter a man. It would make all men think alike, or smother their conviction in silence. Were all men Quakers or Catholics, Unitarians or Baptists, there would be much less diversity of thought, character, and life; less of truth active in the world than now. But Christianity gives us the largest liberty of the sons of God, and were all men Christians after the fashion of Jesus, this variety would be a thousand times greater than now; for Christianity is not a system of doctrines, but rather a method of attaining oneness with God. It demands, therefore, a good life of piety within, of purity without, and gives the promise that whoso does God's will, shall know of God's doctrine.

In an age of corruption, as all ages are, Jesus stood and looked up to God. There was nothing between him and the Father of all; no old word, be it of Moses or Esaias, of a living Rabbi or Sanhedrim of Rabbis; no sin or perverseness of the finite will. As the result of this virgin purity of soul and perfect obedience, the light of God shone down into the very deeps of his soul, bringing all of the Godhead which flesh can receive. He would have us do the same;

worship with nothing between us and God; act, think, feel, live, in perfect obedience to Him; and we never are *Christians* as he was the *Christ,* until we worship, as Jesus did, with no mediator, with nothing between us and the Father of all. He felt that God's word was in him; that he was one with God. He told what he saw—the Truth; he lived what he felt—a life of Love. The truth he brought to light must have been always the same before the eyes of all-seeing God, nineteen centuries before Christ, or nineteen centuries after him. A life supported by the principle and quickened by the sentiment of religion, if true to both, is always the same thing in Nazareth or New England. Now that divine man received these truths from God; was illumined more clearly by "the light that lighteneth every man"; combined or involved all the truths of Religion and Morality in his doctrine, and made them manifest in his life. Then his words and example passed into the world, and can no more perish than the stars be wiped out of the sky. The truths he taught; his doctrines respecting man and God; the relation between man and man, and man and God, with the duties that grow out of that relation, are always the same, and can never change till man ceases to be man, and creation vanishes into nothing. No; forms and opinions change and perish; but the Word of God cannot fail. The form Religion takes, the doctrines wherewith she is girded, can never be the same in any two centuries or two men; for since the sum of religious doctrines is both the result and the measure of a man's total growth in wisdom, virtue, and piety, and since men will always differ in these respects, so religious *doctrines* and *forms* will always differ, always be transient, as Christianity goes forth and scatters the seed she bears in her hand. But the *Christianity holy men feel in the heart*—the Christ that is born within us, is always the same thing to each soul that feels it. This differs only in degree and not in kind, from age to age and man to man; there is something in Christianity which no sect from the "Ebionites" to the "latter day saints" ever entirely overlooked. This is that common Christianity, which burns in the hearts of pious men.

Real Christianity gives men new life. It is the growth and perfect action of the Holy Spirit God puts into the sons of men. It makes us outgrow any form, or any system of doctrines we have devised, and approach still closer to the truth. It would lead us to take what help we can find. It would make the Bible our servant, not our master. It would teach us to profit by the wisdom and piety of David and Solomon; but not to sin their sins, nor bow to their idols. It would make us revere the holy words spoken by "godly men of old," but revere still more the word of God spoken through Conscience, Reason, and Faith, as the holiest of all. It would not make Christ the despot of the soul, but the brother of all men. It would not tell us, that even he had exhausted the fulness of God, so that He could create none greater; for with Him "all things are possible," and neither Old Testament or New Testament ever hints that creation exhausts the creator. Still less would it tell us, the wisdom, the piety, the love, the manly excellence of Jesus, was the result of miraculous agency alone, but, that it was won, like the excellence of humbler men, by faithful obedience to Him who gave his Son such ample heritage. It would point to him as our brother, who went before, like the good shepherd, to charm us with the music of his words, and with the beauty of his life to tempt us up the steeps of mortal toil, within the gate of Heaven. It would have us make the kingdom of

God on earth, and enter more fittingly the kingdom on high. It would lead us to form Christ in the heart, on which Paul laid such stress, and work out our salvation by this. For it is not so much by the Christ who lived so blameless and beautiful eighteen centuries ago, that we are saved directly, but by the Christ we form in our hearts and live out in our daily life, that we save ourselves, God working with us, both to will and to do.

Compare the simpleness of Christianity, as Christ sets it forth on the Mount, with what is sometimes taught and accepted in that honored name; and what a difference. One is of God; one is of man. There is something in Christianity which sects have not reached; something that will not be won, we fear, by theological battles, or the quarrels of pious men; still we may rejoice that Christ is preached in any way. The Christianity of sects, of the pulpit, of society, is ephemeral—a transitory fly. It will pass off and be forgot. Some new form will take its place, suited to the aspect of the changing times. Each will represent something of truth; but no one the whole. It seems the whole race of man is needed to do justice to the whole of truth, as "the whole church, to preach the whole gospel." Truth is entrusted for the time to a perishable Ark of human contrivance. Though often shipwrecked, she always comes safe to land, and is not changed by her mishap. That pure ideal Religion which Jesus saw on the mount of his vision, and lived out in the lowly life of a Galilean peasant; which transforms his cross into an emblem of all that is holiest on earth; which makes sacred he ground he trod, and is dearest to the best of men, most true to what is truest in them, cannot pass away. Let men improve never so far in civilization, or soar never so high on the wings of Religion and

Love, they can never outgo the flight of truth and Christianity. It will always be above them. It is as if we were
to fly towards a Star, which becomes larger and more bright
the nearer we approach, till we enter and are absorbed in its
glory.

If we look carelessly on the ages that have gone by, or
only on the surfaces of things as they come up before us,
there is reason to fear; for we confound the truth of God
with the word of man. So at a distance the cloud and the
mountain seem the same. When the drift changes with the
passing wind, an unpractised eye might fancy the mountain
itself was gone. But the mountain stands to catch the
clouds, to win the blessing they bear, and send it down to
moisten the fainting violet, to form streams which gladden
valley and meadow, and sweep on at last to the sea in deep
channels, laden with fleets. Thus the forms of the church,
the creeds of the sects, the conflicting opinions of teachers,
float round the sides of the Christian mount, and swell and
toss, and rise and fall, and dart their lightning, and roll their
thunder, but they neither make nor mar the mount itself. Its
lofty summit far transcends the tumult; knows nothing of
the storm which roars below; but burns with rosy light at
evening and at morn; gleams in the splendors of the mid-
day sun; sees his light when the long shadows creep over
plain and moorland, and all night long has its head in the
heavens, and is visited by troops of stars which never set,
nor veil their face to ought so pure and high.

Let then the Transient pass, fleet as it will, and may
God send us some new manifestation of the Christian faith,
that shall stir men's hearts as they were never stirred; some
new Word, which shall teach us what we are, and renew us

all in the image of God; some better life, that shall fulfil the Hebrew prophecy, and pour out the spirit of God on young men and maidens, and old men and children; which shall realize the Word of Christ, and give us the comforter, who shall reveal all needed things. There are Simeons enough in the cottages and Churches of New England, plain men and pious women, who wait for the Consolation, and would die in gladness, if their expiring breath could stir quicker the wings that bear him on. There are men enough, sick and "bowed down, in no wise able to lift up themselves," who would be healed could they kiss the hand of their Saviour, or touch but the hem of his garment; men who look up and are not fed, because they ask bread from heaven and water from the rock, not traditions or fancies, Jewish or heathen, or new or old; men enough who, with throbbing hearts, pray for the spirit of healing to come upon the waters, which other than angels have long kept in trouble; men enough who have lain long time sick of theology, nothing bettered by many physicians, and are now dead, too dead to bury their dead, who would come out of their graves at the glad tidings. God send us a real religious life, which shall pluck blindness out of the heart, and make us better fathers, mothers, and children; a religious life, that shall go with us where we go, and make every home the house of God, every act acceptable as a prayer. We would work for this, and pray for it, though we wept tears of blood while we prayed.

Such, then, is the Transient, and such the Permanent in Christianity. What is of absolute value never changes; we may cling round it and grow to it forever. No one can say his notions shall stand. But we may all say, the Truth, as it is in Jesus, shall never pass away. Yet there are always some even religious men, who do not see the permanent element, so they rely on the fleeting; and, what is also an evil, condemn others for not doing the same. They mistake a defence of the Truth for an attack upon the Holy of Holies; the removal of a theological error for the destruction of all religion. Already men of the same sect eye one another with suspicion, and lowering brows that indicate a storm, and, like children who have fallen out in their play, call hard names. Now, as always, there is a collision between these two elements. The question puts itself to each man, "Will you cling to what is perishing, or embrace what is eternal?" This question each must answer for himself.

My friends, if you receive the notions about Christianity, which chance to be current in your sect or church, solely because they are current, and thus accept the commandment of men instead of God's truth—there will always be enough to commend you for soundness of judgment, prudence, and good sense; enough to call you Christian for that reason. But if this is all you rely upon, alas for you. The ground will shake under your feet if you attempt to walk uprightly and like men. You will be afraid of every new opinion, lest it shake down your church; you will fear "lest if a fox go up, he will break down your stone wall." The smallest contradiction in the New Testament or Old Testament; the least disagreement between the Law and the Gospel; any mistake of the Apostles, will weaken your faith. It shall be with you "as when a hungry man dreameth, and behold, he eateth; but he awaketh, and his soul is empty."

If, on the other hand, you take the true Word of God, and live out this, nothing shall harm you. Men may mock, but their mouthfuls of wind shall be blown back upon their

own face. If the master of the house were called Beelze-
bub, it matters little what name is given to the household.
The name Christian, given in mockery, will last till the
world go down. He that loves God and man, and lives in
accordance with that love, needs not fear what man can do
to him. His Religion comes to him in his hour of sadness,
it lays its hand on him when he has fallen among thieves,
and raises him up, heals, and comforts him. If he is crucified, he shall rise again.

My friends, you this day receive, with the usual formal-
ities, the man you have chosen to speak to you on the highest of all themes,—what concerns your life on earth; your
life in heaven. It is a work for which no talents, no prayer-
ful diligence, no piety, is too great; an office, that would
dignify angels, if worthily filled. In the eyes of this man
be holden, that he *cannot* discern between the perishing and
the true, you will hold him guiltless of all sin in this; but
look for light where it can be had; for his office will then
be of no use to you. But if he sees the truth, and is scared
by worldly motives, and *will* not tell it, alas for him! If
the watchman see the foe coming and blow not the trumpet,
the blood of the innocent is on him.

Your own conduct and character, the treatment you offer this young man, will in some measure influence him. The
hearer affects the speaker. There were some places where
even Jesus "did not many mighty works, because of their
unbelief." Worldly motives—not seeming such—sometimes deter good men from their duty. Gold and Ease have,
before now, enervated noble minds. Daily contact with men
of low aims takes down the ideal of life, which a bright
spirit casts out of itself. Terror has sometimes palsied

tongues that, before, were eloquent as the voice of Persuasion. But thereby Truth is not holden. She speaks in a thousand tongues, and with a pen of iron graves her sentence on the rock forever. You may prevent the freedom of speech in this pulpit if you will. You may hire you servants to preach as you bid; to spare your vices and flatter your follies; to prophecy smooth things, and say, It is peace, when there is no peace. Yet in so doing you weaken and enthrall yourselves. And alas for that man who consents to think one thing in his closet, and preach another in his pulpit. God shall judge him in his mercy; not man in his wrath. But over his study and over his pulpit might be writ— EMPTINESS; on his canonical robes, on his forehead and right hand—DECEIT, DECEIT.

But, on the other hand, you may encourage your brother to tell you the truth. Your affection will then be precious to him; your prayers of great price. Every evidence of your sympathy will go to baptize him anew to Holiness and Truth. You will then have his best words, his brightest thoughts, and his most hearty prayers. He may grow old in your service, blessing and blest. He will have

> "The sweetest, best of consolation,
>   The thought, that he has given,
>   To serve the cause of Heaven,
> The freshness of his early inspiration."

Choose as you will choose; but weal or woe depends upon your choice.

Note on the Texts

The problem of a correct text for the three discourses reprinted in this volume is not so simple as one might suppose. In every case, the commonly received text has been edited by other hands since the death of the author and does not represent either his original version or his final revision. In Parker's case, corruptions of the text which crept in almost a century ago have been copied in successive reprints ever since.

After preaching at Sparks' ordination, Channing lingered in Baltimore for the remainder of the week, revising the manuscript for publication. Just how the revised version differed from the spoken address, we cannot determine. There is a manuscript copy in the possession of the American Unitarian Association, but it seems to be a rough first draft, rather than the text as he had it with him in the pulpit. Channing's handwriting was not always as clear as it might have been, so that a number of errors were made in the first Baltimore edition; these were reproduced in the unauthorized Boston edition.

The authorized Boston edition doubtless presents a text that Channing had approved. A decade later, however, when the sermon was included in Channing's *Discourses, Reviews, and Miscellanies* (1830), a good many minor alterations were made, especially with respect to punctuation. The sermon was again reprinted, in 1841, in the third volume of Channing's collected works. This text continues some of the altered punctuation of the 1830 version, but it returns in certain respects to the original text. In spelling and punctuation it is, perhaps, the most acceptable version for modern readers of all the early editions, even though the punctuation in more recent reprints has been further revised.

We know that, in reading his address, Emerson made minor alterations in the text before him. Elizabeth Peabody wrote long afterwards, in her *Reminiscences of William Ellery Channing,* that there was a passage in the original manuscript warning against making new truths a fanaticism; this passage Emerson omitted for lack of time. When she urged him to include it in the printed version, he demurred, stating that it would not be fair to those who had criticized the address to seem to shift his ground in any way. The first edition, we may therefore assume, presents the text substantially as it was delivered.

In 1849, when Emerson printed a volume called *Nature, Addresses, and Lectures,* he made a number of stylistic improvements. There remained, however, certain idiosyncrasies of punctuation that offended James Elliot Cabot, who was responsible for the "Riverside Edition" of 1884. Cabot's text, with some further minor emendations, has resulted in the familiar Centenary Edition of 1903.

The manuscript for Parker's sermon was given a careful revision before it went to the printer. In a prefatory note, however, the author indicated that the alterations were stylistic only and that no modifications had been made in the doctrines as originally enunciated. Since his orthodox listeners were unable to find in the printed text some of the offensive language that they were certain had been uttered, they immediately accused him of suppression. In rebuttal Parker printed, as an appendix to the second edition, more than eight pages of variant readings, so that his critics might reconstruct the original manuscript if they chose to do so. Parker's variant readings served to demonstrate three things: that the three orthodox ministers had heard a number of things Parker had never said; that the differences between the manuscript and the printed text did not affect the substance of the sermon; and that he had polished his text with great care, like the craftsman of words that he was.

The sermon was reprinted unchanged in 1843 in a volume called *Critical and Miscellaneous Writings.* It was again reprinted in 1864 in the London edition of Parker's works, edited by Frances Power Cobbe. This time, however, the text was carelessly handled. The punctuation was altered; Parker's capitalization in such phrases as "Religion of the Pulpit" and "Religion of the Street" was not respected; and the word "revelations" in the second paragraph came out "relations." Since this edition has been the basis for later reprints, including the Centenary Edition (1908), it is obvious that we have been using a text that does not represent Parker's exact intentions.

The following versions have therefore been used for the present reprint: the Baltimore Sermon, from Channing's *Works* (1841); the Divinity School Address, from Emerson's *Nature, Addresses, and Lectures* (1849); and the South Boston Sermon, from Parker's *Critical and Miscellaneous Writings* (1843). In this way, the revisions made by the authors themselves have been respected, but alterations made by later editors have been eliminated.

think abt Emerson - if you think of God as
external to self then refusing to take
respons. for own actions

can alw lk fr help outside self instead
of lking for inner strgth to carry thru